KALEIDOSCOPE

SUFFOLK

Edited by Carl Golder

First published in Great Britain in 1999 by
POETRY NOW YOUNG WRITERS
Remus House,
Coltsfoot Drive,
Woodston,
Peterborough, PE2 9JX
Telephone (01733) 890066

HB ISBN 0 75430 427 2
SB ISBN 0 75430 428 0

FOREWORD

This year, the Poetry Now Young Writers' Kaleidoscope competition proudly presents the best poetic contributions from over 32,000 up-and-coming writers nationwide.

Successful in continuing our aim of promoting writing and creativity in children, each regional anthology displays the inventive and original writing talents of 11-18 year old poets. Imaginative, thoughtful, often humorous, *Kaleidoscope Suffolk* provides a captivating insight into the issues and opinions important to today's young generation.

The task of editing inevitably proved challenging, but was nevertheless enjoyable thanks to the quality of entries received. The thought, effort and hard work put into each poem impressed and inspired us all. We hope you are as pleased as we are with the final result and that you continue to enjoy *Kaleidoscope Suffolk* for years to come.

CONTENTS

Breckland Middle School

County Upper School

Hannah Kilner	71
Philip Blowers	72
Gemma Block	72
Craig Green	73
Lorna Peck	74
Elisabeth Van Dijl	75
Abby Hunt	76
Andrew Moss	76
Rachel Rardin	77
Louise Martin	78
Fiona Berry	78
Stephen Charles	79
Kevin Holliday	79
Stella Barry	80
James Gray	80
Martin Arnold	81
Adam Herrick	82
Hayley Moss	83
Melissa Rudderham	84
Philip Daniels	84
Becka Thomas	85
Emma Curry	86
Debbie Gough	86
Rachel Cox	87
Chloë Shanahan	88
Jody Parry	88
Sheree Hartwell	89
Ellen Cotterell	89
Naomi Rogers	90
Rachel Bates	90
Julie Ranu	91
Polly Spicer	92
Mark Chamberlain	92
Sally Baxter	93
Roxanne Boatright	93
Becci Davies	94

Hadleigh High School

Alison Calkin	94
Nicky Rae	95

Ipswich High School

Elizabeth Marchant	96
Victoria Godley	96
Caroline Beaton	97
Charlotte Davitt	98

King Edward VI School

Jennifer Parkes	98
Lisa Tippett	99
Ciara Corrigan	100
Sarah Byford	100
Rebecca Williams	101
Camilla Wilcock	101
Matt Howard	102
Rachel Blackburn	103
Gemma Willcox	104
Claire Burgess	105
Emma Hilder	106
Lindsay Johnson	107
Joanne Foyster	108
Liz Walden	109
Delaney Mabry	110
Kevin Johnson	111
Sophie Lightfoot	112

Leiston High School

Sarah Winyard	112
Stuart Last	113
Ben Peskett	114
Hayley Shimmon	115
Gemma Nuttall	116
Rebecca Ellis	117
Chris Pflaumer	118
James Lapwood	119

Claire Edmed	120
James May	121
Stuart Pegg	122
Lee Goddard	122
Daniel Mann	123
Elizabeth Smith	124
Raymond Garlick	125
Lisa Sillett	126
Veronica Pearce	127

St James CE Middle School, Bury St Edmunds

Joe Rennison	128
Kurt Smith	128
Althea Tester	129
Ashley James Browne	130
Lizzie Gillard	130
Ryan Theobald	131
Adrian Easton	132
Helen Sanderson	132
Alex Reed	133
Donna Burlingham	133
Holly Youles	134
Laura Duchesne	134
Lee Moye	135
Sam Welsh	135
John Warren	136
Willy Marsden	136
Daisy Tayler	137
Danny Bowles	137
Hannah Fensom	138
Kelly Bryant	138
Ashley Ruffles	139
Nicholas Hazelton	139
Emily Sim	140
Daniel Hopkins	140
Daniel Whittaker	141

The Poems

VANISHING BOOK

I open my eyes,
And look to see
A black cat is to be,
I look at it
And point my stick,
It turns its head,
I wave my stick,
It looks at me,
I watch it move.
Then I cast a spell
Which was to tell,
Mary, Mary,
Quite contrary
Change my book
Into a fairy.
Whales' tails,
Snails' slime,
Old man's toes,
A petal from a rose,
A pig's nose
And a bit of garden hose,
I tell the spell once,
Again then I hope to see,
No book in front of me.

Laura Byles (11)
Breckland Middle School

THE SCREAMING WOODS

The woods are misty.
It was thundering as I walked through
I heard screaming.
Footsteps coming towards me
I ran and hid behind a tree
I saw two eyes of flame
And I saw a shadow
Coming towards the tree
I heard an echo and
I saw a big nose and I saw
Blue lips and I ran
And ran, it ran after me.
I looked behind me, it wasn't there
I ran and ran until I got home.

Paul Wake (12)
Breckland Middle School

MY PET BLACKIE

My cat Blackie's totally black,
He runs around the house,
Chasing a little brown mouse,
He eats chunky brown meat,
Which is his little treat.
He walks around the garden,
With his head hung high.
He even chases butterflies.
When he's angry,
He flicks his tail in the air,
And hovers around everywhere.

Jeanette Marsh (12)
Breckland Middle School

FEELINGS

It makes you feel happy,
All the romance makes you feel like you're floating on a bed of clouds.
When you say the word *love*, it makes me think of sweets.

Anger is miserable,
It feels so depressing,
It makes you feel like you're six feet underground.
When someone says the word *anger* I think of bombs going off
everywhere
And I also think of spicy mustard.

I love surprises,
Surprises are usually happy,
They jump out of boxes and cakes,
They make you jump when you least expect it.

I hate sadness,
It's so depressing,
You just want to curl up in a ball and die.
I'm never going to feel sad again.

Rachel Hodder (12)
Breckland Middle School

THE BRAINY LIQUID

Add all these together
And stir up some trouble
Ten toenails, three rusty nails and a couple of snails.
Stir them up in a ten foot cauldron
And 'puff'! It makes you brainy
But that's not all
Eight of your fingers and a couple of black ink markers.
Then all of a sudden I get a twitch
Oops! I forget I'm a witch.
But it doesn't work straight away
It takes a few days.
But instead of failing, I'm getting A's
This liquid only lasts for a few days.
So you need a
Flick of my nose
And a kick of my toes
And then I know
How to do my
Maths, English and Science
For a few days I've been using this liquid and now I' not
so great.

Leanne Marriott (11)
Breckland Middle School

No Man Knows

Five men's finger nails,
Three men's toes,
Seven male eyeballs
One packet of tomato soup.

Hippty hop,
Lippity lop,
Turn this bald man into a mop!

An old dusty rubber,
A tin of dead mice,
One rusty pencil tin
And an old man's bin.

This turns a bald man into a mop that is on legs,
So men can do all the mopping up.

Carman Kent (11)
Breckland Middle School

Freak From The Moon

My friend Fred is a freak from the moon.
He landed in a spaceship in the shape of a spoon.

With his little red horns and his green scaly skin,
I looked quite boring compared to him.

He has freaky powers, he drinks through his nose.
He sleeps on his head and breathes through his toes.

I said, 'Goodbye,' to my green scaly friend.
He zapped off in his spaceship never to see me or Earth again.

Jennifer Clarke (12)
Breckland Middle School

SPELL FOR A STORM

Five human toes,
A witch's nose,
Eyes of a mouse,
Mould from a house,
A frightening crash,
Burnt old ash.
But still there is worse
For my enchanting curse.
My curse shall create a storm,
Very, very cold, not warm.
With creepy, crawly, horrible slugs
And terrible spine-chilling bugs.
Oh gather round my cauldron pot.
Don't get too close, it's rather hot.
It is the colour
Of scarlet red
The heat will soon
Get to your head
So little children
Go to bed and wait for my *s t o r m!*

Jessica Miller (11)
Breckland Middle School

A SPELL TO . . .
BE A WITCH

Three toad noses,
Seven bat wings,
One hundred purple pumpkins,
Fifty-three dolphin fins,
To turn me into a witch.
Seven glaring eyes,
Slugs and bugs,
Mice and rats,
Cats and dogs,
And not to mention my best friend's arm
My own big toe!
I will drink and eat my spell all night
And turn into a witch by sunset.

Fiona Hinton (11)
Breckland Middle School

FACTS ABOUT BOYS

Boys are disgusting, dirty creatures,
They pick their noses and backchat teachers.
If you can't find them outside playing football,
They are usually in the bathroom squeezing a pimple.
They pick on girls with frizzy hair or funny curls.
They have greasy hair,
When it comes to work they don't really care.
The other day there was a whole pot of gel,
Now it's on his hair to impress a girl,
If she has any sense she'll say, 'Go to hell!'
    Boys
        Boys
            Boys

Claire Matthews (12)
Breckland Middle School

HORROR STORY

Beware, you're in for a scare.

A dark, scary, foggy night
Thunder booming in the soggy forest
All mist around trees and bushes rustling
Evil eyes hiding behind the crunchy barked tree
Watching me walk along the noisy bank.
Making noises around me, whistling and rustling
I walk on and on getting scared. I turn around.
Footsteps thumping along -
A blue sharp light appeared in the tree.
As I look a werewolf appeared
All hairy with big sharp teeth, big pointy ears.
Staring and glaring at me, walking towards me
With his big sharp claws swinging.
I pull out my flame-thrower, I start shooting
Growling with anger
Drooling, dripping down
The sun begins to rise, while the werewolf disappears.

Jason Spooner (12)
Breckland Middle School

GHOST TOWN

Up I jump in my bed
I wonder if the noise
Is just in my head
No, it's not, I can hear a rattle
Is it just Mum and Dad
With their tittle tattle?

I get out of bed
I look out of the window
I hear another sound
I lean further out
I look further around
I see a ghostly figure
I look back
I scream and say
It's like a ghost town.

Natalie Field (11)
Breckland Middle School

DREAMER

When you fall asleep,
and it's very, very deep.
Your dreams will come along,
and sing you a dreamy song.
Some dreams are good,
Some dreams are bad,
Some dreams are happy,
Some dreams are sad.
People can dream of monsters in their back yard
who come in the kitchen and eat all the lard.
Dreams can be of anything
like flying through the sky.
You could be a murderer
or a dead guy.
Dreams when you're sleeping
Dreams in the day
Dreams, dreams never go away
Dreams, dreams they're here to stay.

Khalid Bilal (12)
Breckland Middle School

GRAN LOVELL

Gran Lovell
A 100 years old
Sitting round the fire
Telling stories
Sack round her back
A cup of tea in her hands
A clay pipe in her mouth
Has a gift with horses
Wrinkled and toothless
Gold earrings
Hang from both ears
Shining like the sun
On a hot day
Made mistletoe
And holly wreaths
No more, for her hands
Were too shaky.

Nicola Lynam (11)
Breckland Middle School

A SPELL TO MAKE YOU BETTER AT ENGLISH

A wing of a bat
A bathroom tap
A forgotten mat
A gentleman's top hat

An ear of a cow
A snout of a sow
A smelly old boot
And a tatty old flute

Hubble bubble and all that trouble,
So there you have your spell.
In English you shall do well,
Now try and spell,
I hope you do well.

Rachel Clarke (11)
Breckland Middle School

ON THE WAY ENGLAND

Sitting in the waiting room,
Everyone there,
The silence is too much for me to bare.
As we sit there waiting for the plane,
I look around and see my family and friendly faces all fill with pain,
'Cos we're leaving,
Going to a new land
Called England.
I'm leaving all my friends
Starting anew.
What if I don't like it, then what will I do?
I've got to be strong,
Life goes on.
The time has come to move on.
Away from America we go.
Will I see them again?
I don't know.
I already miss them and I'm not even gone,
I wish my dad could come too.

Brittany Meyer (12)
Breckland Middle School

SCHOOL SPELL

This is a spell to make school disappear,
No more shouting *'Are you here?'*
This is what you have to say,
To make the school go away.
Rulers bend before my eyes,
Teachers rise up to the sky,
Rubbers, books, pencils and pens,
Rise before I count to ten,
Blackboard go away right now,
Rules and lessons take with you,
Pow.
A wave of my wand,
A wink of my eye,
A tap of my stick and say 'Bye bye.'

Lisa Coote (12)
Breckland Middle School

GRAN LOVELL

Gran was 100 years old
She has a hat on
And wears big earrings.
Her cheeks are red
She cooks all the time
She smokes a pipe
Gran told stories next to the fire
With the children round her.
She died under the wagon.

Michael Lane (11)
Breckland Middle School

THE TRAMP

He sits in the doorway of Woolworth's
Waiting for people to come,
Wanting his hat to be filled with gold
Though this will never be done.

He finally decides to shift himself,
Away from the busy crowds,
'Where shall I sleep?' he asks himself
Who knows, who cares?

He thinks to himself, who wants me?
'No one,' came the silent reply,
He should be used to it now
He's had it all his life.

He curls up in a corner,
Getting ready to sleep,
He falls asleep, freezing cold,
With things crawling at his feet.

It's morning but he doesn't wake,
No one really cares,
Born a tramp you die a tramp,
There's no one there to care.

Alicia Cox (13)
Breckland Middle School

BUNNIES

I looked at all the bunnies,
And they all looked a little funny,
A fluffy little tail,
That's all curly and pale,
Floppy, big ears,
That look like giant tears,
And little tiny eyes,
That look like mini pies,
And when they hop along,
They look a little oblong,
They're smaller than a log,
But bigger than a frog,
They all look cute and cuddly,
But some are a little fussy,
They're all soft and sound,
In their little crowd.

Rebecca Hinton (12)
Breckland Middle School

DIFFERENT

Being different
Sure is weird.
All the kids laugh,
Laugh at me.
Sometimes I laugh,
Sometimes I cry.
It sure feels weird being different.

I have two friends,
That are just like me, different.
Sometimes I laugh,
Sometimes I cry.
It sure hurts having it all,
All bottled up inside.

They laugh at me because they don't know,
Know what I know.
They sit and make fun of me,
But I know that I can trust
My two best friends.

Kids can be cruel,
But they can also be nice.
Maybe if I keep my hopes up high
They will like me.

Melissa Ryfa (13)
Breckland Middle School

HUNGRY

In front of you are . . .
Fat, juicy, greasy chips
Sizzling, burnt sausages
Mashed, dumped upon the plate.
Baked beans travelling around the chips
And the drink is Coke, bubbling in the glass
But I'm standing outside.
Watching in surprise
Wondering if I will even have the chance.
Easter alone,
Christmas alone.
I'm all alone on the street
With no shoes on my feet
No one is there to pick me up
When I'm feeling down.
But I know that I will die one day.

Tina Betts (12)
Breckland Middle School

MONSTER

Some monsters are different sizes
Some monsters come with little surprises.
Some monsters have long ears,
Some have small,
Some monsters grow to the top of my hall.
I found one yesterday in my living room,
But when he saw me he flew off with a *zoom!*
When he flew into a tree,
He picked up a stick and threw it at me.
He didn't like to be laughed at by me,
That's why the stick stung like a bee.
He flew away out of sight,
And he did give me quite a fright.
I want to meet him again soon,
But he only comes when there's a full moon.

Phillip Morgan (12)
Breckland Middle School

HORROR POEM

Willows whistle, moonlight shining
bark crackling.
Flash of light flashed through
the trees.
Deeper into the woods,
My pulse pumping faster and faster
Zigzag in and out of the trees
Under and over, ducking and diving.
Sunlight gleamed in my eyes.

Tanya Field (12)
Breckland Middle School

MYSTERY CREATURE

I walked into the woods.
Three minutes later it became
dark and gloomy.
It started to rain.
I ran back, but I didn't
go the right way.
I came to a graveyard.
As soon as I stepped
on to the yard a
great big thunderbolt
hit the ground.
I saw a shadow.
I heard strange sounds.
My heart started
pounding against my chest.
I saw two red circles
with a hole in the middle,
they came closer
and closer.
I ran, I heard a growl.
Then I heard a leap, I
turned. The strange creature
was right over me, he
looked like parts of
different animals.
Aarrgghh!

Daniel Hartley (12)
Breckland Middle School

AFRICA

In Africa there are,
Cheetahs running 100 mph and over.
Crocodiles waiting in the water for lunch to come to his door
Vultures and hyenas waiting,
Waiting for the lion to finish its kill
A leopard in a tree with a gazelle.
Once again the vultures and the hyenas are there.
Gazelle and the wildebeest eating grass.
Some keep watch while others eat.
One has spotted a lion
Run, run, run
One less wildebeest to the herd.
But next time it could be someone else
It's a fact of life in
Africa.

Lee Hodson (12)
Breckland Middle School

FRIENDS

Life can be boring
Life can be sad
But when I'm with you
You make me feel glad

When it's hard
You help me through
But sometimes we have
A harsh moment or two

Give me that cake,
Throw it here,
It's all your fault

So when it comes to friends
You're the best mate

So go on give me that cake!

Jade Collinson (12)
Breckland Middle School

AEROPLANE

An almighty roar as the plane takes off
The plane flies high above the sky above the clouds
The seats so comfortable and smooth
The ride so quick and graceful
All you can hear is the roar of the twin engines
The ground below you so tiny and small
The different lights of New York
The huge mountains in the Himalayas
The destination is in sight
The plane begins to descend
Your tummy goes up and down
The runway is clear
We suddenly brake and the plane screeches to a halt
We get out of the plane
What a relief!

Ben Woods (12)
Breckland Middle School

LADY

As a lady walks past
with a slimy slippery coat,
she makes the men stare
as she climbs into her £80,000 boat.
She says, 'Peter put your foot down.'
As they speed off over the turquoise water
Peter hit his head on the ceiling.
He says, ' I wish I was a little shorter.'
The lady looks posh
as she's dealing out cash.
The driver loses control
and the boat went *crash!*
The man was alive,
the lady lying in disbelief,
the money was all wet
as she was dying like a leaf.
The man was helping her
as the ambulance had arrived.
Peter put on his coat and said,
'It's too late, she's died.'

Arron Frewer (12)
Breckland Middle School

GHOST HOUSE

In his bed he lay there wet,
Completely drenched in his own sweat.
In his bed he lay there still,
Sheets pulled over his head.
He called out once but heard no reply,
He called out twice, three times and four,
Would he have to call out any more?
Before he heard any reply.
Once again he heard someone move,
This time closer and moving still.
He moved back slowly,
Clenching his sheets in his hands.
Once again he called out,
This time louder and more scared than before.
This time though he heard a reply,
A little girls voice, soft and sharp.
He pulled the sheets back and there he saw,
At the foot of his bed a little girl of six, no more
All of a sudden she turned her back and skipped away,
Her soft, sharp voice calling no more.

Thomas Chichon (12)
Breckland Middle School

THE PUPPY

The puppy sits there,
Cold and tired. Cowering in the corner,
Away from any danger.

Away from the
Human eye.
He curls up in his,
Cardboard box.

No food to eat,
No water to drink.
No warm rug to lie on,
No hands to lick.

He just sits there and
Watches the world go by.
He wants someone to
Love him, someone to care.

No one wants him,
This is what happens.
People craze for a pet
But soon get fed up.
Animals are left at the
Side of the road for no
Fault of their own.

Mary Revell (12)
Breckland Middle School

TRAMP

He is furry and scruffy,
You wouldn't have thought that,
His name is not Bill or Tom,
His name is simply Tramp.
Because,
He's a cat,
He leaps and jumps
And dances about,
He chases his prey for miles,
Until he hears his dinner shout,
He looks up,
And then runs off.

He jumps on to the fence,
And then in his house,
He eats his dinner, along with a mouse.
He jumps up and walks to his owner,
He jumps on her lap,
He settles down swiftly,
For a short nap.

He now wakes up,
Stares at the floor,
What woke him up?
He walks to the door,
Miaows for ages, nobody comes,
Finally it opens,
The cat's let out,
The door is locked,
Now he's shut out.

Jennifer Taylor (12)
Breckland Middle School

NINE MONTHS

Baby brothers and sisters,
They take too long
And they're only a mess,
It's hardly worth the wait!

The first month of the nine,
Your mum is worried if the baby's alright.
The second month is the one that your mum's in the
hospital all the time.
The third is the month that your mum feels fat and very
heavy.
The fourth is the one your mum gets to see the baby,
How exciting!
The fifth is definitely the worst,
Your mum gets sick.
The sixth is the one you want to call it quits,
Who wants a baby anyway?
The seventh is the month your mum takes classes,
Just to learn how to breathe,
The eighth is awful,
All you do is wait, wait and wait!
But after all of that you come to the ninth,
That's the best,
The baby comes!

Joanne Rainey (12)
Breckland Middle School

DESERT ISLAND

Desert Island, oh so lonely,
Sitting all by yourself,
Nobody comes to see you any more,
Where is all your wealth?
Could you change yourself,
To make people come again,
Instead of having to put up with lonely beaches?
The loneliness you feel inside,
It's obvious you cannot hide.
When people fly above you,
All they see is an empty space,
What an awful waste.
This world is full of people,
That don't accept a thing,
This world could begin,
To learn to use good again.
The world will come to you,
Don't shed a single tear.
Relax and take a rest,
Calm your restless water,
No ship will ride your waves.
Save yourself my friend,
Your life will never end.
This world will come to you.

Stevie Pease (12)
Breckland Middle School

GUESS IT IF YOU CAN?

Guess my animal if you can:
He's cute and furry
With big paws too
He can live anywhere in the world
His ears are tufty as can be,
His eyes are big and brown
He hunts alone
No friend in the world
He's more lively at night
In the day he hides away
In a cave he makes no sound because the hunters are around
If he saw you he would run
Away to the bushes till the break of day
Have you guessed him?
If you haven't,
He is a . . .

Dale Marriott (12)
Breckland Middle School

HORROR POEM

I wandered through the misty woods.
Shimmering light came from the moon.
I was cold and damp.
I was scared, my frustration got bad,
My pulse was pumping like mad.
But all of a sudden my
Blue light flashed like lightning.
I was scared and I didn't know what to do.
Then all of a sudden my pulse was running.

Hayley Neal (12)
Breckland Middle School

TWILIGHT ZONE

Evil twilight
Beating trees
Thunder booming
All around.
Star lights here
Evil eyes here and there
Brown hair, pointed ears
Screaming echo here and there.
Flashing light
Losing breath
Gritting teeth here and there.
Evil eyes with a beam
Of light beaming
Towards you.

Craig Leon (12)
Breckland Middle School

THE GLOOMY NIGHT

The evil creature.
Evil glare.
Frantic red eyes,
Grey, wrinkled evil creature
Gritting teeth fangs in mouth
Walking behind me
Footsteps like thunder.
Anger was in the storm.
It wanted revenge.
The footsteps were still there
And before I noticed
There were eyes of flame
I ran and the storm became gloomy.

Mark Parsons (12)
Breckland Middle School

THE HOMELESS

Lying there on the street
With mud and dirt at his feet

No money, no friends
Not a care in the world
He sits in a ball all tight and curled

Never a job, never a home
He's sleeping in a garden with a bag for a dome

No blanket, no pillow for him on to rest
To cover his tatty old torn vest

In winter he's wet and muddy as can be
In summer he's hot and lays under a tree

Day by day, night by night
As the years go by he puts up a fight

Fighting illness, fighting death
Fighting pain as he slowly loses his breath.

Dean Macleay (12)
Breckland Middle School

THE LONER

There he is again sitting on the bench,
no one that cares and no one that shares,
his problems about his life,
he has no family not even a wife,
not one soul talks to him,
he's known as a weirdo,
which isn't very nice,
people just ignore him,
and snub him from their lives,
he sits there through winter,
he sits there through spring,
he doesn't really care what happens to him,
what will become of this poor lonely man,
nobody knows,
and nobody cares.

Michelle Pearson (12)
Breckland Middle School

THE LONER

Over a hill and under a sky
Lives a man with just one eye
He's a normal man of normal sorts
Of normal shirts and normal shorts
All day long he dreams of gold
And all those stories he once told
His children have gone, their children have left
All that remains is his life and his death
The moral of this story, which I propose
Is to look at the dwelling that which you have chose
Try to make sure that your family live by
And remove all sharp objects which could take out your eye.

Alex Wood (13)
Copleston High School

THE MOON

This is a place where a deep sea diver
Swims without water.
A place to stare,
A bar that closes for lunch.
Gonna fly to the moon
Later rather than soon.

Thursday morning is really night,
Ghosties come not to give you a fright,
Instead of cars you drive in kites
Gonna fly to the moon
Later rather than soon.

Rules of the game
Run while you walk
Be quiet when you shout
Eat soup with a fork
Gonna fly to the moon
Later rather than soon.

Alison Larke (13)
Copleston High School

MY WORLD

Climb the tree upside down,
Fly by saucepan into town.
Have a bath in a puddle,
Give the pepper mill a loving cuddle!

Taste the music,
Write with a crabstick.
Listen to the photo,
See with a yo-yo!

Kick the habit,
Ride on a rabbit.
Swim like a brick,
Take the mick!

Take a drive in a cupboard,
Paint old Mother Hubbard.
Dust the baby,
Catch ya later - maybe!

Adele Trenter (13)
Copleston High School

EVERYONE

Everyone loves movies,
       movies are the best.
Best friends laugh together.
       Together is how we should be.
Be free, not locked up,
       Upside down is how I feel.
Feel the hurt and the strain.
       Strain the pasta.
Pasta for dinner.
       Dinner is something you need.
Need, everyone needs it.
       It looks like you.
You need someone.
       Someone needs things.
Things for everyone.
       Everyone loves movies.

Victoria White (14)
Copleston High School

MRS ANIMALS

These are a few creatures,
Each with different features,
Their different ways,
Take up the days,
Maybe they can teach us!

My name is Mrs Monkey,
And I am really funky,
I swing in trees,
But mind the bees,
The stings can be real chunky!

My name is Mrs Cat,
And I like it just like that!
I lick my paws,
And clean my claws,
And I always stay and chat!

My name is Mrs Bunny,
And I hop rather funny,
If there's a breeze,
I sometimes sneeze,
And my nose gets rather runny!

My name is Mrs Giraffe,
And I love to have a laugh,
My neck is long,
But I am strong,
And I love my baby calf!

These are a few creatures,
Each with different features,
Their different ways,
Take up the days,
Maybe they can teach us!

Hayley Haden-Scott (13)
Copleston High School

A 'RIESEN' FOR EXTRA CHOCOLATE!

I gaze into the *Galaxy*
And hear a little *Wispa*
I *Drift* into a *Twirl*
And the *Flyte* begins
What if the universe
Was made of chocolate?
I think to myself.
I'd take *Time Out* to explore
Explore the unknown
Fuse together *Dairy Milk*
and *Caramel* to form a
Picnic of *Celebrations*
Neptune could be *Mars*
And
Earth *Milky Way*
Instead of rain *Flakes*
of *Roses* would fall
Quality Streets of
Marble
And for me a *Bounty*
Of paradise
A crisp, a *Crunchie*
Perfect world this would be
What if the world was made
of chocolate . . . ?
I think to myself.

Sophie Arvanitidou (14)
Copleston High School

BUS STOP

Bus stop
Don't go,
On your marks,
Ready, steady,
Cook!
Ainsley Harriot - superchef!
Gorgeous chocolate cake,
Rotten teeth,
Dentist's chair,
Sofa bed,
Sleepy head,
Brain power,
Watts,
Light bulb,
2 lips,
Make-up,
Friends,
Enemies,
War,
Dead.

Johanna French (14)
Copleston High School

MATHS - A STUDY IN A CARAVAN

There once was a maths teaching man
Who did Pythagoras in his old caravan
He found his quotient
Was rather quite potent
Until his inky Y intercept ran.

Luke Scoffield (13)
Copleston High School

ANYWHERE WILL DO

They seem to
live everywhere.
Anywhere will do, the land
the skies or oceans
will do.
Anywhere.
They skim across the
water, glide across
the land, float through the
air at night watching man.
They seem to be
everywhere. Anywhere will do,
eating and surviving
just like me and you.
Birds live everywhere
anywhere will do.
Imagine life without
them I cannot, can you?

Rachel Smy (14)
Copleston High School

JUMBLE!

They think it's all over when it's raining cats
and pigs might look on the bright side
of the yellow brick road,
but a cat has lost one of its nine lives
when Dorothy and Tin Man come down the road.
Don't put all your eggs in people's glass houses
because a bird in the hand shouldn't throw stones
for a stitch is worth two in the bush!

Nicola Finbow (13)
Copleston High School

DREAMS

When I wake up in the morning
I open my curtains to see a lovely scene.

The people sitting in the park
feeding the birds before work.
The milkman on his rounds
sneakily giving milk to a cat.

I walk out onto my balcony
and they all look up and say 'Hello!'

Then I wake up and open my curtains
to a dirty and smelly alley way.

Well, there's no harm in dreaming.

Natasha Emmamdeen (14)
Copleston High School

THROUGH THE EYES

Through the eyes, I can see
Some cheese climbing up a tree.

In the distance, there can be found,
A chair spinning round and round.

A hill is roasting on a fire,
Whilst dragons rule the whole empire.

Through the eyes,
Weird and wonderful things are found.

You were there,
Walking upside down.

Laura Lucock (13)
Copleston High School

IMAGINATION

Use your imagination,
And who can tell,
You could be an air pilot,
Or a manager of a hotel.

A busy, buzzy bee,
A bird flying high,
A whale in the ocean,
Now you have a try.

A graceful ballerina,
Or ride a motorbike,
Live on a desert island,
Over mountains, go for a hike.

I could be an elephant, and bathe in the sun,
Or a hippopotamus, in the mud, having fun.

Just use that little head of yours,
And who knows where you'll be,
But, just for now, I think,
I'll stick to being me.

Harriet Naylor (13)
Copleston High School

PROFESSOR FROM NORWICH

There was a professor from Norwich
Who couldn't stop guzzling porridge
He got really fat
And spluttered and spat
Now he can't fit in his college.

Chris Bristo (12)
Copleston High School

STEP OUT UNDERNEATH THE SKY TONIGHT

As he walked he heard the sound,
And thought someday he'd turn around,
And see the things he'd always said,
We'll hear the thoughts inside his head.

He said one day he'd have it all,
The voices of the world will call,
He claims he made the words he spoke,
And all the reams of joy he wrote.

He speaks his mind and has his say,
Who else commands respect this way,
He lives on talent, on self belief,
Then pulls the diamonds from beneath.

He spoke about the time he'd find,
The brilliance that could flow from his mind,
Just for those who thought he'd miss,
The hand that rocks the cradle's his.

His worries, fears and pains dissolve,
His hands all around the world revolve,
His memories, dreams and plans for all,
Still lie behind his Wonderwall.

Charles Cormack (16)
Copleston High School

TEACHERS

Teachers come in different types
Happy, snappy or mean
Some are cool
Some are dumb
But we don't care how they come!

Teachers come in different styles
Snazzy, smart or messy
Some wear skirts
Some wear suits
But we don't care how they come!

Amir Uddin (13)
Copleston High School

WIND CHIMES IN THE BREEZE

W aving to and fro
I nsecure in the wind
N oisy but peaceful
D reamy moods and

C hilly winds, make
H eavenly breezes.
I   t illuminates the skies and
M akes people's lives tranquil,
E legant and calm,
S ome people know them to be -

I   rritable, others insist they are
N   eat and imaginative.

T   ransforming melodies into
H   armonious tunes that are
E ffective and welcoming.

B affling beats
R acing at speed
E ndless icy draughts
E ngulfing its surroundings
Z esting the environment
E nding in a gentle sway.

Clare Talbott (16)
Copleston High School

ROUTINE POEM

Stress machine moving,
Repeating over again,
Bending over backwards in formation.

Repetitive, boring and sometimes annoying,
Tension flowing freely
In a world that never cares.

Even though we're individuals
We all need each other's help,
Just cogs in a wheel that goes around.

Work, school, college etc.
We've all got these demons in our life.
Live with them, hate them or really learn to make do,
The routine. Has it struck *you*?

Matthew Fitch (13)
Copleston High School

FOOD FIGHTS

Food fights in the dinner hall,
Food fights at home,
Make sure you're not in the way,
When the sprouts hit home.
Yukky semolina, lumpy and thick
Custard, yoghurts, mousse,
And all covered in sick.
Make sure you're not in the way
When the meatballs hit home.
'Cause if you're in the dinner hall when the food fight starts,
You know you'll never come out with a clean shirt.

Sarah Lower (12)
Copleston High School

RING, RING

When the phone rings I beg and I pray,
that the caller on the end will just go away.

It's probably Carly,
she talks for an hour,
I could be doing something worthwhile,
I could be having a shower.

It could be Maria,
not a word of English she speaks,
she's lived here for years,
though you'd think it had been weeks.

Perhaps it'll be Mother,
complaining about Dad,
'He does nothing round the house,'
They both drive me mad.

One of these days I'll pull the plug and never hear that phone,
No nutty friends or insane parents *or* that dreary tone.

Amy Dobrucki (14)
Copleston High School

THE GARDEN

The garden is a lovely place,
that brings a smile upon your face,
the sun shines brightly through the trees,
and flowers dance around your knees.
And if you listen carefully,
you can hear the humming bees,
they fetch and carry honey,
and only wished it could be money!

Chantelle Reed (12)
Copleston High School

IN CASE OF FIRE!

In case of fire, break glass.
In case of glass, fill with water.
In case of water, turn off tap.
In case of tap, answer the door.
In case of door, exit to freedom.
In case of freedom, leave your prison.
In case of prison, window bars.
In case of bar, go for a drink.
In case of drink, a glass of water.
In case of water, put out fire.
In case of fire, break glass.
In case of glass, open window.
In case of window, frame of wood.
In case of wood, put logs on fire.
In case of fire, break glass.

Rachel Reeve (15)
Copleston High School

BIRTHDAYS

B irthdays are brilliant!
I f it's a school day, watch out!
R ight day for a birthday
T oday's the day!
H opefully it comes in the weekend.
D ay you were born.
A lways adventurous and funny!
Y onks of waiting for what you want
S aturdays are best for birthdays.

Matthew Dickerson (12)
Copleston High School

A HALLOWE'EN NIGHT

It was Hallowe'en on an autumn night,
All the zombies came out to fight,
All boys and girls tucked up in bed,
Because the zombies were trying to pull off their heads.

Witches and potions,
And lots of explosions,
Happen on Hallowe'en night.

Trick or treating,
And lots of eating,
While Dracula turns into a bat,
And ghosts scare the witch's cat.

This all happens on a Hallowe'en night.

Jamie Pearson (11)
Copleston High School

I HATE SCHOOL

As soon as I wake up from bed,
the thought of school swirls in my head.
Homework, homework, everywhere,
why do teachers set it? It's just not fair.
Just as I arrive in school,
I imagine the food in the dinner hall:
Stir fried eyeballs and mashed up worms,
the sort of foods that make you squirm.
I reach for the school gate
in an awful state.
Until I realise . . . it's Saturday,
I'm safe.

Victoria Range (12)
Copleston High School

HEARD IT ON THE RADIO

It's like the knot you can't get out of your hair
It's like the goop you can't wipe off your shoe
It's like the stain you can't get out of your top
It's like the homework that you don't want to do.

It's like the Blu-tack that's ground into the floor
It's like the annoying catch on your longest nail
It's like the mascara that makes your eyelashes clump
It's like the exam that you know you're going to fail.

It's like the letter that you're still waiting to receive
It's like the cold that makes you feel really low
It's really annoying, it stays in your head,
That song on the radio.

Debbie Hayes (14)
Copleston High School

BROTHERS

Brothers, they're a pain in the butt,
They're monsters creeping around you,
They're hiding everywhere,
They're in every nook and cranny,
Oh brother!
Is there a way out?
If there is I can't find it,
If there's help I need it,
Oh brother!
Brothers you can't live with them,
And you can't live without them.
Oh brother!

Michelle Baker (12)
Copleston High School

AUTUMN IS HERE

Autumn is here, bright colours everywhere,
Green, yellow, red and orange leaves,
Slowly dropping to the ground,
Crackling, crunching and crumpling underfoot.
Dark evenings start to come around,
Leaves swirling all around,
As the wind whistles through branches,
Trees sway back and forth,
Children running, playing,
Rolling around in the leaves,
As raindrops start to come down,
Dropping off leaves and glistening in the autumn sun.
Early in the morning, all is quiet,
Just the sound of whistling in trees,
As time goes by all leaves are gone,
Trees are bare and the sun has gone.
Winter arrives, the cold is here,
The snowflakes fall and cover all the trees,
And soft white snow is all around,
For a while it's like time stands still,
With an air of loneliness there.
Spring then returns with a glow,
The trees start to stretch and grow,
To the highest height
And luscious green leaves come back into sight.

Luke Ramirez (14)
Copleston High School

I AM . . .

I am . . .

> Life's constant power,
> The first to jump,
> Ready to take control,
> The last to give in.

I am . . .

> The animal lover of the year,
> Always saying 'How sweet' to other people's pets,
> Laughing all the time,
> Grinning constantly.

I am , . .

> A trusting friend,
> A unique species,
> Always thinking of nothing and everything,
> The power of the group.

I am *Me!*

Helen Pratt (11)
Copleston High School

ANSWERS

There are lots of answers to be found
but you don't just pick them off the ground.
Some have to be thought through logically,
but they don't just come to you.

You can read a book and look them up,
or do some sums then add them up;
maybe look inside a cup,
but they don't just come to you.

You can ask a teacher, ask a mate,
maybe someone at your gate.
Be a fisher's bait,
but they don't just come to you.

Listen to your favourite song,
sit in a chair all day long,
thinking what's gone wrong,
then the answers should come to you.

Louise Fairs (14)
Copleston High School

TEN TO NONE

Ten tiny ducklings paddling in a line
One drowned in the water then there were nine.
Nine little boys jumping over a gate
One fell and broke his neck then there were eight.
Eight local people waiting on a train to Devon
One of them fell on the track then there were seven.
Seven pretty girls putting on their lipsticks
One stuck it in her eye then there were six.
Six naughty boys went for a drive
One got caught with alcohol then there were five.
Five groovy grannies dancing on the floor
One did the splits by mistake then there were four.
Four giggling Teletubbies all needed a wee
Po fell down the toilet then there were three.
Three giddy school girls bent down to tie their shoes
One tipped over and banged her head then there were two.
Two hard policemen were shooting with their guns
One got his head blown off then there was one.
One lonely bird flying towards the sun
It got burnt because it flew too high then there were none.

Lizzy White (11)
Copleston High School

WE'RE ALL HUMAN

People are different in many ways,
They maybe young or old in their days,
Black faces and white faces everywhere,
Lots of racism, life's just not fair,
We can't help looking the way we do,
What we believe in and where we're from too,
People come from so many different places,
It's hardly surprising to see different faces,
Accept people for who they are,
Wherever they're from, near or far.

Earth will soon be fighting with war,
They will be killing each other, even the poor,
Fighting over things like religion and land,
I really think war should be banned,
Family and friends dying in pain,
Their living friends will probably go insane,
It's so painful, being cut into bits,
And being burnt and being thrown into pits,
Hopefully war will change over the years,
And release people of their greatest fears.

Nurun Nessa (11)
Copleston High School

MY FOREVER FRIEND

She's like the sister I never had,
She cares for me (although she's mad!)
She's always there when I need to talk,
Appearing from nowhere like a hawk.

I still remember the day we met,
We said a few words and our friendship was set.
11 years on and we're still the same,
Helping each other and dreaming of fame.

We've had our arguments, over the years,
But we sort them out, so that there are no tears.
I really don't know what I would do,
If we were to stop talking for a week or two.

Friend, you know I would die for you,
So let our friendship always be true.
Make sure that we stick together,
So that our friendship goes on forever.

Emma Church (14)
Copleston High School

10 TIDDLY TODDLERS

10 tiddly toddlers talking to wine,
one talked too much then there were nine.
9 nuns talking about being late,
one nun blew herself up then there were eight.
8 enormous elephants sitting in heaven,
one fell down then there were seven.
7 silly snails picking sticks,
one fell down a hill then there were six.
6 sizzled sausages sitting in a hive,
one fell out then there were five.
5 fish fingers stuck to a door,
one fell off then there were four.
4 fat frogs needed a wee,
one wet his pants then there were three.
3 old ladies locked in a zoo,
a lion ate one then there were two.
2 toddlers eating a bun,
one ran away then there was one.
1 wildebeest writing a bill,
he went to post it then there were nil.

Ben Baker (11)
Copleston High School

THE MAN

The man polluted the seas,
The man discovered cures,
The man created war,
The man invented cars.

The man chopped down the trees,
The man worked out the impossible,
The man created crime,
The man invented television.

The man invented good things,
The man created bad things,
The only problem is,
That both of them exist.

Helen Catchpole (13)
Copleston High School

SNAILS ON TOAST

I dared my best friend to eat snails on toast,
She said she would if they were fresh from the coast,
I said 'Ok,' but that was only a joke,
She ate the snails till she nearly choked,
You could hear the shells go crunch, crunch, crunch,
To tell you the truth it put me right off my lunch.
She tried to swallow a big one whole,
But it came back out and hit the cat's bowl.
A dreadful sight, I tell you, it was,
She said they were nice but would go better with rice.
She then said, 'It's your turn now to have a try,'
I said, 'I can't and would rather die!'

Victoria Robins (11)
Copleston High School

ON THE TELLY

My family likes to watch the telly,
Me and Mum and Aunty Nelly,
Uncle Tom just goes to sleep,
When Les Dennis goes 'Beep beep.'

Lenny Henry goes to town,
Carol Vorderman on Countdown,
Fifteen to One, The Price is Right,
One in a Million every night.

You've Been Framed, I really laugh,
At all the people being daft,
Changing Rooms, oh what a sight,
All the colours are too bright.

There's painting, gardening and cooking too,
With Ainsley showing us what to do,
Vets In Practice, look after your pets,
And Animal Hospital you can't forget.

Of all the programmes that I see,
HangTime is the one for me,
Deering Tornadoes are the best,
This show is better than the rest.

Holly Taylor (12)
Copleston High School

STRESSED TEACHERS

There was once a man who had one ear
When he blew it off he shed a tear
Then his wife left him for a younger man
Then he had plastic surgery and called himself Dan.

Ciaran Kennedy (12)
Copleston High School

CHINESE WHISPERS

Kelly started off with 'Frogs, fig, frown, food, frown.'
Who passed it to Leanne,
Who passed it to Jenny,
Who passed it to Sarah,
Who passed it to Carmelle,
Who said aloud, 'Dogs dig down dude, down.'

Next time Leanne started off with, 'House, hi house, hole, hi hole,
hi honey, hust, hake, honey.'
Who passed it to Jenny,
Who passed it to Sarah,
Who passed it to Carmelle,
Who passed it to Kelly,
Who said aloud, 'Mouse, my mouse, mole, my mole, my money
must make money.'

Next time Jenny started off with, 'Sheepy sat, sought sheepy scrawly'.
Who passed it to Sarah,
Who passed it to Carmelle,
Who passed it to Kelly,
Who passed it to Leanne,
Who said aloud, 'Creepy cat caught creepy crawly.'

Next time Sarah started off with 'Gig, glue, gins, Gerri guns.'
Who passed it to Carmelle,
Who passed it to Kelly,
Who passed it to Leanne,
Who passed it to Jenny,
Who said aloud, 'Big blue bins bury buns.'

Next time Carmelle started off with, 'Link, lie, longs.'
Who passed it to Kelly,
Who passed it to Leanne,
Who passed it to Jenny,
Who passed it to Sarah,
Who said aloud so simply, 'Pink pie pongs.'

Sandy Phillips (14)
Copleston High School

SWEET AND PROPER TO DIE FOR YOUR COUNTRY?

I sit alone and wonder why,
I'm the only soldier left to cry.
A tear drops to the floor,
In remembrance of a friend no more.

The mud is thick and waist high,
As the ending draws so nigh,
The drowning bodies sink down deep,
May their souls the good Lord keep.

Then they come over the trench,
And with muscled arms do wrench,
In the Nazis' hands now,
As I become a helpless POW.

Now in Auschwitz my sadness stronger,
Only saying not much longer,
Led to furnace one by one,
In this death camp life is gone,

As my skin begins to fry,
I remember the sick old lie,
When we were made to see,
'Dulce et decorum est pro patria mori'.

Peter Garner (15)
Copleston High School

A School Day

Starting on time,
Corridors jammed.
Hurrying to classes,
Opening the doors.
Oh, no! Bell's gone
Late again!

Talking and chalking
Every night, homework.
Always demanding,
Challenging and moaning.
Hearing every whisper
Even out of class.
Resting in the staff room
Some hope of peace!

Hard work,
Odious,
Mental torture,
Every day.
Working hard,
Over and over.
Racking our brains,
Kicking our heels.

Paul Gooding (13)
Copleston High School

The Kitten

The kitten so playful
Would sleep and often peep
Anywhere under a chair
Especially a radiator
He doesn't care.

The kitten, he came in a cardboard box
Then hid in the cupboard
With all Mum's frocks.

Sophie Mursell-Head (11)
Copleston High School

TEN SLEEPY TEACHERS

Ten sleepy teachers, standing in a line.
One went to hide in the bathroom, then there were nine.

Nine sleepy teachers, all their pupils late.
One stormed off in anger, then there were eight.

Eight sleepy teachers, dreaming of heaven.
One did not wake up, then there were seven.

Seven sleepy teachers, each eating their 'Pick 'n' Mix'.
One was poisoned, then there were six.

Six sleepy teachers, doing the jive,
One collapsed with exhaustion, then there were five.

Five sleepy teachers, walking down the corridor.
One was kidnapped, then there were four.

Four sleepy teachers, demonstrating the knee,
One pupil tested the teachers' reflexes, then there were three.

Three tired teachers found a smelly shoe,
One fainted of the pong, then there were two.

Two sleepy teachers, eating a currant bun,
One started choking, then there was one.

One sleepy teacher, not having any fun.
So he gave up his job and went home, then there were none.

Jessica Scoffield (11)
Copleston High School

MY TEACHER

I climbed up a mountain
all covered in sand
I shot my poor teacher
with a rubber band
I shot her with courage
I shot her with pride
For I could not miss her
She was 50ft wide

I went to her coffin
She wasn't quite dead
So I got my bazooka
And shot off her head

I went to her funeral
I went to her grave
People threw flowers
I threw a grenade

I got a new teacher
His name was Mike
I did not like him
So I got my bazooka
And blew up his bike.

Samantha Martin (14)
Copleston High School

MY FRIEND MONSTER

I used to know a monster
He liked to go out and sing,
But people used to throw things at him
And call him 'the thing'.

One night he sat on a wall
And someone thought he was a cat,
So he went outside and skinned him alive
And used him as a mat.

Natasha Ely (12)
Copleston High School

HOLIDAYS

Having holidays going abroad,
That's what most families can afford.
That's what going away is all about,
It gives you a reason to scream and shout.
Away from home, away from school,
Lying a thousand miles away by the pool.
Swimming deep in the sea,
While Mum sunbathes under a palm tree.
At the disco, music blaring,
Whom I'm with, I'm not caring.
Moving with the constant beat,
Dancing so much I can't feel my feet.
The next day sending postcards away,
Telling my friends how much I'd love to stay.
Now just days before we depart,
Leaving here would break my heart.
But it won't though,
Because when I go,
I'll have a home to use,
And nothing to lose.
Because one day I'll return,
With more to learn
About this same destination,
God's most beautiful creation.

Cara Davies (12)
Copleston High School

MY LIMERICK

There was an old man called Bill,
Who worked at Sainsbury's Till,
He did something wrong,
The bell went ding dong,
He was forced to sit down for a pill.

Samantha Whittaker (11)
Copleston High School

ME

Inside me there is a lion,
ready to leap out.
It crouches down,
its prey in sight
and Mum comes in and
turns out the light.

Christopher Hubbard (12)
Copleston High School

I AM . . .

I am the disco jiver,
I am the mouth of gods,
I am the bookworm reader,
I am the rain, stars and sun,
I am the world turning, whirling,
I am the sea waving, twirling,
I am the trees sprouting new leaves,
I am the millennium.

Amelia Minns (11)
Copleston High School

YO-YOS!

Yo-yos, yo-yos everywhere,
Yo-yos in the playground,
Yo-yos in the air.
Yo-yos in the classroom,
Yo-yos on the seats,
Yo-yos in our school and
Yo-yos in the streets!
Yo-yos, yo-yos doing tricks,
Yo-yos broken needing a fix.
Yo-yos, clutches, gears and springs,
Yo-yos sleeping, climbing up strings.
Yo-yos, yo-yos in everyone's head,
Tamagotchis at home, all of them dead!
Yo-yos, yo-yos, the latest craze,
Yo-yos, yo-yos, they're here to stay!

Nuzhah Ali (11)
Copleston High School

INSIDE ME

Inside me there is a rainbow of colours,
Blacks, browns and dull colours,
For unhappy moments,
Tigers, lions and dragons come out with these colours,
Rage, roar and growl with anger,
Yellows, purples and blues for happier days,
Out come butterflies, clear blue skies and birds,
Sweetly singing and gracefully flying,
When sadness comes,
Dreary greys and dark blues,
Animals hunch up and slowly walk,
Heads down looking at the ground.

Bethany Dale (11)
Copleston High School

THE LITTLE MONSTER

There's a little monster in my house,
He creeps around at night
And when I'm asleep in bed
He gives me such a fright.

Early in the morning,
The monster creeps around
He pulls my hair and chews my pens
Then makes an awful sound.

I know the little monster's name
And so does my mother
The horrible thing, I'm afraid to admit
Is that the monster is my brother.

Kathryn Arnold (11)
Copleston High School

INSIDE ME

Inside me
there is a zip of excitement
a dash of colour
and a fizz of happiness.
It bubbles in my fingers
it bubbles in my toes
it bubbles all around me
even in my nose.
Also in me there is a fearsome tiger
which roars when I'm cross
and purrs when I'm not
that is the end of inside me
now I'm going to climb a tree!

Elise Dixie (11)
Copleston High School

A TYPICAL WEDDING DAY

A typical wedding day goes like so:
Bride wakes with major hangover,
Only five hours left to go.
Mother's knocking on the door,
'How are you feeling? How's the head?'
Bride wishes she'd stayed in bed.

A typical wedding day goes like so:
Groom wakes with monster hangover,
Only two hours left to go.
Best man's knocking on the door
'Hope you remembered to iron a shirt!'
Groom's head is beginning to hurt.

Hair,
Make-up,
Jewellery,
Nails,
Bride takes ages to prepare.
TV,
Fry-up,
Top hat,
Tails,
Groom considers washing his hair.

A typical wedding day goes like so:
Two Bentleys make their way to church,
It's ten to two and traffic's slow.
The light turns green, the race is on,
Both parties are now fit to burst,
The question is: who'll get there first?

Jemma Hale (14)
Copleston High School

BEING LOVED

I am the worn CD
All day spinning and turning,
My beat driving through
The body of the dedicated listener.
My words slicing and tugging on his heart,
Expressing my innermost feelings towards him.
The grooves of my shiny body
Are worn down to a smooth finish.
Bored, dizzy, feeling sick,
Oh, the pain of being loved so much.
I feel tired and lonely.
Hoping one day I will be put back
In my plastic coffin
With the inlay card.
I like being loved, of course I do.
But, not as much as this!

Rafaele Reeve (14)
Copleston High School

FUNNY THINGS

A bottle of wine is a funny thing you know,
How quickly in my house one seems to go.
Is it the flavour, dry or sweet?
Or is it the sophistication that is so unique?

Chocolate is also a funny thing you know,
How quickly in my house it all seems to go.
Is it the flavour, milky or plain?
Or is it the creaminess that drives us insane?

Louise Atkinson (14)
Copleston High School

CLICHÉS

If I win the lottery,
You'll have to come to terms with it.
I'll make a keynote speech,
(And not moan like an old woman)

Education, education, education,
I'll make a man of him,
For school days are the best days of your life
(But, doesn't life start at 40?)
You'll have to learn the hard way,
If you're as young as you feel,
Time is a good healer.
Women are so emotional,
But big boys don't cry,
And, it will be alright on the night.

Hannah Jacobs (15)
Copleston High School

MY TRAINER IS . . .

My trainer is Puma
  My trainer is old
My trainer is comfy
  My trainer is cool
My trainer is tatty
  My trainer is one
My trainer is everything I need to
                    Run!

Rebecca Hart (12)
Copleston High School

A Poem About Love

Hearts
blessed
friend
more
realisation
life touched
peace, happiness
kind forgiveness
given so much
good thing
one
right beside me
feels right
mystery.

Lucy Spurling (15)
Copleston High School

Love

Love, what's it all about?
Is it kissing under a tree?
Is it long walks by the sea?
Is it asking someone to marry you
on one knee?
Is it something you say
just to please?
Oh God tell me, is it
kissing under a tree?
Is it long walks by the sea?
Is it asking someone to marry you
on one knee?
Oh God, please tell me.

Sarah Byam (13)
Copleston High School

THROUGH THE STAFF ROOM DOOR

Ten tired teachers drinking some wine,
one had too much then there were nine.

Nine angry teachers marking work they hate,
one fainted of stress that left eight.

Eight freaked teachers falling asleep,
one went to heaven then there were seven.

Seven bored teachers hoping the bell won't go,
one had a bag of pic 'n' mix that left six.

Six lonely teachers standing in the class,
one doing the jive then there were five.

Five lazy teachers dreaming in their own world,
one came smashing through the door that left four.

Four hippie teachers standing by the lockers,
one saying peace to a tree then there were three.

Three annoyed teachers standing in a line,
one saying eye, eye, to the crew that left two.

Two talkative teachers getting a sore throat,
one ate an iced bun then there was one.

One smelly teacher writing on the board,
I'm having a baby son, that left *none!*

Emma Smith (11)
Copleston High School

THE DARK

The dark, the dark,
it happens at night.
When I was younger,
it gave me a fright.

Mum, Dad! I used to shout,
leave the light on,
don't put it out!

Creeping shadows around my room,
was it a ghost,
or a witch on her broom?

Hiding under the duvet,
shaking with fright,
Go away dark,
hurry up light.

Michael Taylor (13)
Copleston High School

THE PRIME MINISTER

There once was a man called Blair,
Who was rapidly losing his hair!
British Prime Minister was he,
And leader of the Labour Party.

Tony Blair has a very cheeky grin,
Against his rivals he did win.
The Conservatives he kicked out,
And the Lib Dems he forgot about.

Now Downing Street is his home,
For five years he will roam.
Or maybe longer,
If the others don't get stronger.

His cabinet he often shuffles,
To iron out the ruffles.
He's still plenty to learn,
Until he finishes his term.

Gavin Pooley (13)
Copleston High School

HORROR ON THE DANCE FLOOR

The school bell rings
The weekend begins
In three hours I have to be there
So now it's time to wash my hair
It's time to put my glad rags on
And dance to my favourite songs.
I'm ready to get up on my feet
As I hear the music beat
I pull my friends up on the dance floor
As I hear the speakers roar
Then the lights begin to dim
And various people start to sing
I start to dance without a care
Then to my horror my trousers tear
The lights come on and people stare
It's not my fault, I have holes in my flares.

Katie Read (15)
Copleston High School

WHERE DO THEY GO?

Why do things always disappear in our household?
I think they move of their own accord,
Or perhaps it's an invisible spirit,
That creeps around the house silently,
Moving things from place to place.
But where do they go?
Dad's glasses' case often vanishes,
And turns up in the most unusual places,
'I'm sure I left it here!' he'd say,
Scratching his head,
Thinking hard.
But where do they go?
It's also a puzzle,
That the wine in the kitchen
Rapidly decreases like water,
From the beginning of the evening
Till later.
Wonder why?
My sisters are just as bad.
'Where is that top?'
They yell at the top of their lungs.
'I can't find anything to wear!'
But where do they go?
I suppose I should face it
That there are some things we have all lost:
Our marbles!

Martha Burley (12)
Copleston High School

AN ODE TO MY TEACHER - MR PEARCE

One day whilst playing netball at school
I decided to take a heavy fall,
My sports mad teacher Mr Pearce
Tried to console me when I shed tears.

My body started to tremble and shake
The day my ankle decided to make a clean break,
The teachers thought it was only a sprain
But if only they were in my pain.

The office staff quickly phoned my mum
And in a panic along she ran.
I did not find this very much fun
Oh Mr Pearce! If only I had a gun.

Off to casualty we did go
The waiting time was ever so slow,
But at last X-rays were taken
And my poor foot was aching and breaking.

After my leg was put in a plaster cast,
I was allowed home on crutches at last,
But my dancing career is now on hold
And as for netball, well! I must be bold.

Now this saga is coming to an end
I hope Mr Pearce will make amends
And finally realise what he has done
By putting an end to all my fun.

Samantha Nice (12)
Copleston High School

ELEGY FOR AN UNEDUCATED WASP

Wilfred Wangleton Waverly Wasp
Was a wasp of dignity and pride.
He tried to learn how to read a book
But this is how he died.

She stalked her prey with the stealth of a cat
And has an eye to where her victim is at
The smirk on her face when she saw her prey
Increased the poor little wasp's dismay.

The frail little wasp buzzing around,
Up in the classroom far off the ground,
Was keen to learn of the wonderful things
In books, the plays and other such things.

The weapon was raised
The heel of a shoe
A dark destroying, deep shade of blue.

Waverly Wasp now starting to panic,
His circling movements increasingly manic.

The whip of the shoe cut through the air
Missing the wasp with inches to spare
As Waverly zigs and zags in the air.

He travelled from far
Over seas of green
And climbed walls of red,
Trying not to be seen.

Because all he had wanted
Was to learn how to read,
He ended up buried
Beneath a green weed.

Nicholas Jinks (15)
Copleston High School

AUTUMN

We see the golden wheat
and lorries carrying muddy sugar beet.

It's time for hot oats
and putting on our winter coats.

The leaves are falling from the tree.
The birds are flying across the sea.

Squirrels are climbing up the oak.
It's raining now and they are soaked.

The snow will come very soon.
So while all the animals get ready to sleep,
We play in the leaves so deep.

Michael Cavanagh (11)
Copleston High School

AMETHYST

Jagged, faceted,
Sharp, smooth,
Irregular,
Heavy in a palm.

Glimmering intricate shapes,
A mountainous landscape,
Transparent purple quartz,
Intensely reflecting light.

Nature's enchantment,
Majestically mesmerising,
Strangely satisfying,
Beyond human capabilities.

Hannah Kilner (13)
County Upper School

THE SHELL

It was thick at the bottom getting thinner as it curled to the top
As long as an ice-cream cone but with no ice-cream or flake
Walking along the golden sandy beach on a scorching summer's day
And there it lay
Half buried in grainy sand by the small salty rock pools
Thick swirls swirling round and round to the top getting smaller
and smaller
Cream, ivory white
Rough when you first touch it
Running your fingers through the deep grooves
I picked it up
As light as a pencil
Questioning the shape of the shell
Weird but wonderful
What once lived in this thing of beauty?
It could fly through the air like a dart or a bullet from a gun
It slithered into my pocket like a snake down a hole
And we walked home.

Philip Blowers (13)
County Upper School

FOUND POEM

An oyster lies on top of the water,
I open the shell,
The muscle tightens as I open it,
And there it lies, the great pearl,
As large as the moon,
Beautiful, rich, warm and glowing,
The greatest pearl in the world.

Gemma Block (13)
County Upper School

MY FAMILY POEM

'Beep Beep Beep!' goes my alarm,
I get up with a yawn
And an ache.
The sun beams through my tightly
Closed curtains as I rise
From my bed.
My fish surface asking
For food, they scurry
As I feed them,
I go down with creaking footsteps
And a waft of toast greets me.
I crunch through my toast
As my brother thunders
Down the stairs.
I go into the bathroom
To brush my teeth,
Amongst the smells of shampoo
And soap, the toothbrush scrapes
Against my teeth
And scratches my gum.
The noise of the car scrunches
Down the drive, Mum shouts
'Come on Craig.'

Craig Green (13)
County Upper School

MY STONE

The shape of an umbrella,
The length of my smallest finger,
The brightest star in the sky,
Lying beside the cliff's edge.

A blue smudge,
Like part of a rainbow.
A white outer crust,
Surrounding a centre of blue.

Dark as the dusk,
I picked it up,
Rough,
With speckles.

Comfortably it sat,
In the palm of my hand,
Not heavy,
But just right.

I wonder how it got there?

Who knows?
Oh well,
Nobody else can find it,
It's mine now!

Lorna Peck (13)
County Upper School

THE SHELL

There it lay
Surrounded by the sea urchins,
Down by the coral reef,

A cone,
Coiled up inside,
Large as my palm,
A crown on top.

I picked it up,
Shaped to the clasp of my hand,
Smooth,
The sea on a calm day.

A subtle shade of yellow,
Reflecting the sunshine beam,
Shining like a pearl,
Perfect.

How did it end up there?
Lying so still,
A secret tunnel,
What's inside?

Placed back,
Onto the sea bed,
Back where it belongs.

Elisabeth Van Dijl (13)
County Upper School

THE SHELL

A horn and a tail,
With a fresh sea smell,
Camouflaged but different.

Lying peacefully,
The shape abandoned,
Alone, and different.

Colours mixed to yellow,
So unusual,
Like something with no meaning.

How did it get there?
Why did I find it?
How is it so different?

The place it was lying,
Was in another world,
Definitely cut off from anything else.

I kept it,
And have never lost it,
It's mine.

Abby Hunt (13)
County Upper School

WHAT'S THE DIFFERENCE

What's the difference
between men and women?
Is there any difference?
Are they equal?

Men do labour work
Women do housework
Men get their hands dirty
Women clean up the dirt

Women do the cooking
Men like take-aways
Men stand back and watch
Women do the vacuuming

What's the difference
between men and women?
Is there any difference?
Are they equal?

Andrew Moss (15)
County Upper School

SEASCAPE

The rolling hills of the sea
attack the shore,
rising up ready to dive
mercilessly on the sand.
Leaping and crashing,
the wind drives them on,
faster and faster.
Then they break.
The gentle foamy waters
lap the edge of the stony beach.
A seagull flies through the
clear blue sky overhead.
Then a lightning streak
and the sky turns a gloomy grey.
The stormy sea roars up in anger
and the winds form a howling gale.
Gulls screech and fly away from the storm.
The storm is forever.
Forever. An eternity.
But finally - calm.

Rachel Rardin (14)
County Upper School

MIRRORS

The light reflects on it
Like the moon on a pitch black night

As you stare at it, it stares back
Your double

Following you wherever you go
Vanished
Behind the solid brown frame

You go to meet her
She walks too
Could you walk through?
Stopped, by the shining light glass
A mirror?

Louise Martin (14)
County Upper School

MIDNIGHT

A city full of people,
Vanishes. Black.
A dead city.
The moon picks out shadows,
Made by passing clouds.
Silence.
The distant sound of an owl,
is all that's heard.
The coldness of the moon,
Shivers.
A big black sheet covered up life.
Dead.

Fiona Berry (14)
County Upper School

DAILY ROUTINE

Pour into empty school
get hot,
remove jumper.
Maths on third floor
seven hours of work,
two hours of homework
pour out of full school,
into empty streets.
Into terraced houses
doors slammed in sequence.
Relax with drink
watch TV until nine.
Pour out of chair
into warm bed.
Drift into dream
routine, routine
routine . . .

Stephen Charles (15)
County Upper School

NATURE IS AMAZING

Nature is amazing
There are so many different things in nature,
There are horses,
There are dogs and a lot more animals.

Nature is amazing
Human beings are part of the natural cyclone,
there are trees
Trees contain lots of leaves and pretty birds.

Kevin Holliday (15)
County Upper School

A SOLITARY OAK

An oak
A solitary being,
Or maybe with a forest of friends.
A splash of colours,
All shades of green, and brown.

A bird.
A lonely bird,
Lands in that solitary oak
A speck of feathers
Within a huge cushion of leaves.

The bird.
It's too lonely in the solitary oak.
Flies off into the crowd
Rejoins its flock of friends
Like the leaves on that solitary oak.

Stella Barry (14)
County Upper School

THE SHELL

Its size is smaller than a pen
It just lies there half-covered in sand
With water lapping onto it
It's a whitish colour
It's shaped as a spiral with small lines in each of the spirals
I pick it up
It's smooth rubbing it one way but then rough rubbing it another
Its past was spent in the sea with others
But its future will be spent on my shelf.

James Gray (13)
County Upper School

SEXISM

Sexism helps the world revolve,
Just like love and peace,
It separates the men and women,
Your nephew and your niece.

Women do the washing,
Men just take life easy,
Scrub that plate real well,
At the moment it's all greasy.

Women do the cooking,
While men read the paper,
Don't go to bed yet love,
I might feel hungry later.

Women do the sewing,
The darning of men's shirts,
And men just watch the TV,
With women in short skirts.

Women take the dogs for a walk,
They regularly clean the loo,
And also do the smelly task,
Of cleaning up doggy doo.

Women get less pay,
Than the men at work,
The simple reason is because,
Her boss is a sexist jerk.

Sexism helps the world revolve,
Just like love and peace,
It separates the men and women,
Your nephew and your niece.

Martin Arnold (15)
County Upper School

THE RED STONE

Two squared edges,
Conker sized,
But not
Conker shaped;
Around the edges,
Are different shades of colour,
Small dents penetrate the surface.
I found it on the beach,
Yet then,
Not a scratch on its beautiful face.

It shines in the light,
A dark vein runs through,
Deeper than
A red traffic light,
A polished surface,
Sparkling bright;
But what lies within,
This wonderful sight?

I picked it up.

Tiny indents,
Smooth,
Not in any way coarse,
With tiny scratches you cannot feel.

Coming from magma,
An igneous rock,
Becoming liquid again,
In a million years' time.

I put it on the windowsill
To be admired.

The red stone.

Adam Herrick (14)
County Upper School

MIRRORS

I'm in a room which seems never-ending,
I see a gun and I need defending.

I can see ten doors, and run for one,
I hit a mirror this game is no fun.

'I'm stuck' I shout but no one hears,
I feel my eyes bulging with tears.

The gun is now being held by me,
Hang on a minute, what's this I see?

There's a light coming from the sky,
What's happening now, why me, why?

The light stops and all goes quiet,
Then suddenly there's a huge noisy riot.

Kids come running in and I know where I am,
I'm at the fair with the dodgems and the big brass band.

I imagined the gun, I imagined the light,
I am now going home, in the dead of night.

Hayley Moss (14)
County Upper School

WHY DO MEN, WHY DO WOMEN?

Why do men place bets
when they know they're going to lose,
And do they have to pick on women
when trying to amuse?

Why do men have egos
the size of the Milky Way,
But women get the blame
For anything they say?

Why do women spend money
on clothes they never wear,
And get uptight and angry
When the men go past and stare?

Why do women eat chocolate
and then moan about their weight,
But when couples go out to dinner
It's the woman who's always late?

So why do men grief women
and women blame the men,
But when both have said they're sorry
they do it all again?

Melissa Rudderham (16)
County Upper School

MIRRORS

Reflecting an image
of a room, twice as big
Shining in sunlight
like a stream on a hill.

Philip Daniels (14)
County Upper School

SADNESS

A small, insignificant in a huge gang,
I am a tall girl, with normal brown hair.
Normal life or so people think.
Inside I am different, a freak many would think,
But sadness and loneliness is serious,
I feel alone and empty
With words in my head:
Why? Me? *Notice my misery!*

I think and talk to myself until I am noticed.
Tears build a wall that is battered down by an eyelash.
People act concerned but they don't really care, not deeply!
I want to be noticed but also left alone
I may still be at school, with hundreds but my mind is one.
One person, one mind, one life but many, many problems.
I can't list them all, some complicated, some not.
I may only be a teenager but my heart and mind are more.

Isn't sadness and depression solo?
I start to think of my old life and friends,
The small village but containing 'my' family and 'my' past.
People that don't think of me but I of them.
I think of my family's problems and the people I have lost.
The dam has now broken and I start a flood of my own tears.
I want to stop writing but I don't really want to
I have wheels turning in my head,
And my thoughts re-appear like the mud of a cart.

I do want a life but would like to be dead,
To have my problems buried along with my sorrow.
One day my sorrow will be no more and I'll soon be forgotten,
No gap left in the fabric.
That makes no sense? But neither does my life.

Becka Thomas (14)
County Upper School

MIDNIGHT

Dark with bright
Stars shining.
Big Ben says the time is twelve.

Wolves howl
Spirits cry
Young children dream
but what about?

Some people call this
The witching hour
I would say the world is sick
Sick with evil.

The sky is black
And has no feeling
It is like a plague
Dark and dismal.

Dull, unfriendly, evil
Just like death!

Emma Curry (14)
County Upper School

LIFE

Life is a mystery
confusing us all
where does it begin
and where does it end?

Picking up the pieces
of all the wrong we do
how do we put it right?
nobody knows.

Having a laugh
having a cry
emotions entangled
how do we put them right?

Life is strange
In a way we don't understand
but that's why we're here
that's life.

Debbie Gough (15)
County Upper School

ARE WE LIKE ROBOTS?

Why are we like robots?
Maybe it's because we do nearly the same thing every day
Some might enjoy it
Others might say we have to, to survive
It is weird how we just do our routine
We get up
We go out to work or school
We come home
We go to bed
And it goes on and on
Until another year goes by
Or someone rebels against this mundane routine
It gets a bit mundane
But deep deep down we love to keep doing it
So, are we like robots?
Some might say yes
Others say no.

Rachel Cox (16)
County Upper School

MIDNIGHT

Midnight,
darkness and emptiness,
a cold breeze,
and the rustling,
of near trees.

Midnight.
The last minute of the day,
and soon today's yesterday.
The morning starts to awake,
It has to be midnight.

Midnight.
Darkness and emptiness.

Chloë Shanahan (14)
County Upper School

WHY?

Why is a woman expected to do everything
yet a man gets away with murder?
Why is it that a woman should have to clear up
after her slob of a husband has created the mess?
Why is a woman left standing at the burning stove
when her husband is down the pub?
Why should a woman look after their children every single day,
while her husband is out drinking throwing their money away?
Why is it that a woman realises this
but lets herself be treated in this way?
Why?

Jody Parry (15)
County Upper School

MIDNIGHT

The wind blows down the
chimney stack.
The howl makes a shiver,
Go down my spine.

I look at the clock,
And it has just struck twelve.
I look out the window
And all I see is darkness,
The moon is the only light,
I see.
A diamond in the sky.

Sheree Hartwell (14)
County Upper School

MIRRORS

Mirrors.
Alone on walls, they hang with pride to show
what we cannot see.

Reflections that are hard and strong stare
back with strength to me.

These shining shapes that still gleam at night
have seen the whole day's looks.

These are the lonely mirrors.

Ellen Cotterell (14)
County Upper School

MIDNIGHT

It was a clear night,
The stars were shining,
The North star, Orion's belt,
The Plough, all shining
Then nothing, all dark.

In the wood at midnight,
I was walking alone,
When suddenly the moon
Broke through the trees.
Full.

It lit everything,
A very strong lightbulb,
I was blind in the dark,
But now I could see
Shadows moving.

A howl came from nowhere,
Then movement in front.
Frozen, I glanced around,
Then nothing,
Stillness.

Naomi Rogers (14)
County Upper School

ETHIOPIA

A country full of starving people.
They cry for help,
But no one answers.
Where will their next meal come from?
Their next meal is someone's leftovers.

Hunger,
Starvation,
Screams of pain
Coming from within.
Cries of fear.

Rachel Bates (14)
County Upper School

THE PAIN OF IVORY

In pain and defenceless,
The elephant lies.
The battle is hopeless,
Under the African skies.
Surrounded by guns,
Then *bang!*

Everywhere is silent,
Not a bird moves.
There on the ground,
The large elephant is still.

In a hiding place at a distance,
The calf sees the lump,
Its mother,
Dead,
Under a tree.

Moments later the hunters are gone.

The babe, just weeks old,
Watches.

It's a high price to pay,
Just, for some ivory.

Julie Ranu (14)
County Upper School

MIDNIGHT

Darkness. Its silence is broken,
by a hooting owl,
or a fast car.
The moon is your only saviour,
the light comforts you, reassures.
The nagging worry of rape,
and murder screams in your head.
An internal fight, in your brain concludes.
You run, run faster,
the silent sound of footsteps echo.
I stop, silence.

Polly Spicer (14)
County Upper School

LETHAL

A gun. Designed to kill
Nothing more, nothing less
The shiny silver bullets, loaded into the barrel
The trigger pulled, the smoke, the bang
The screams of pain, the blood, the horror
Then death.
A gun. Designed to kill.

Mark Chamberlain (14)
County Upper School

MIRRORS

Gazing into the reflecting glass
You see an image
It's looking at you
You move to the left
It moves to the right
You raise one hand
It raises the other
You draw in closer
It draws in too
You stare at it
And it stares at you.

Sally Baxter (14)
County Upper School

LETHAL

A strange type of lethal,
Not a knife or a gun,
Something much more special than that,
Which cannot be taken away,
Or be replaced.
A feeling you get,
No understanding if you have not been there before.
Your own world with one amazing person.

Roxanne Boatright (14)
County Upper School

DANGER!

Danger comes in many ways.
Exciting. Fearful. Suspense.
Exciting danger when you know you shouldn't be doing it.
Fearful danger when you're in the house on
your own and there's funny noises.
Surrounded danger by the thought of
knowing you're going to get caught.

Becci Davies (14)
County Upper School

THE SEA
(An Exercise in the use of Simile and Metaphor)

Calm, still it lay, a vast sheet of turquoise silk,
Spilling gently onto a sherbet shore.
Lapping waves wash silently onto the golden sand,
That rests in the afternoon sun.

The azure plain, sends ripples onto the sapphire fringe shore.
As the tide returns, a shuffle is heard from the shifting shingle.
Hsss, a rustle from the polished pebbles.
And the cool, sea-spray, sprinkles the untouched, mottled shells.

And then, a rip-roaring tide pounds onto the rocks,
Like a tiger pouncing on its prey.
White stallions willingly gallop up the beach,
And a creamy foam ices an uneven cake.

The stones clatter and crash,
As they are tossed by the furious sea.
Then, everything returns to calm,
Like a vast sheet of turquoise silk.

Alison Calkin (13)
Hadleigh High School

THE STORM

The wind frantic, shrieking, whistling
Like a mad man in a hurry
The rain splashing, splattering
Like God was crying
Hailstones thumping at the floor
Thunder roaring and rumbling
Like someone shouting horrendously loud
Lightning ripping as the rain still tumbles
The wild wind and the fierce rain
Making the streetlights smash
Like glass shattering
The lights went out in every house
It was dark
Like the dead of night
The wind got quieter
The thunder and lightning stopped
As if the world stood still
No light, no noise
No thunder, no lightning
Quiet like an empty church
God was at peace.

Nicky Rae (13)
Hadleigh High School

MY AUNTY ROSIE

My aunt is a sweet smelling teddy bear,
Always ready for a big hug,
Or a cry,

She's a mug of cocoa by the fire,
Ever inviting,
Ever pleasing,

My aunt is a delicate mauve and
amber butterfly,
Fluttering and floating in the
midsummer haze,
Ever breezy and kindly beautiful,

She is a blank page in a diary,
Waiting for me to write down
my feelings.

Elizabeth Marchant (11)
Ipswich High School

HOMEWORK

I was sitting in the classroom,
bored, as bored can be,
When suddenly my teacher cried,
'Oh my gracious me.'

She was looking at my homework,
Oh dear I dread to think,
When she sets her eyes on me,
I'll become extinct!

I felt my hands go sweaty,
And my face turn beetroot red,
All my breath was drained away,
I felt so close to dead.

But then she looked up from my book,
And gave a great big smile,
She stared at me in disbelief and said:
'I haven't seen work as good as that in a long while!'

Victoria Godley (11)
Ipswich High School

THE SPIDER

The spider spins her web of silk,
Her legs busily weaving,
She appears to be innocent and friendly
But she is deceiving.

Did you know she catches flies
And pierces them with her fangs?
Then she wraps them up in silk,
And from her web they hang.

Then, when they are surely dead
And the wriggling expires,
She sucks the blood out of the corpse,
Rather like a vampire.

So the spider isn't sweet,
Her cruelty is immense,
And all the flies in your garden will die
If her web is on your fence.

Caroline Beaton (11)
Ipswich High School

To Nigel The Tooth Fairy

Nigel, Nigel you're a hag!
Why is my money on the drag?
Oh, you hurt my feelings so,
I was relying on that dough!
Could it be that you are broke,
Or not a very decent bloke?
I need a fiver for the delay,
I might pay you back one day.

From a deprived child.

Charlotte Davitt (12)
Ipswich High School

Confusion

What to do? What to say?
What did it mean?
Questions, questions but no answers
yet.
Waiting for an explanation.
No opinion on the subject, no say or
input to give.
Not knowing the exact situation
What's right? What's wrong?
What now? Where now from here?
A blank future, nothing to gain,
Nothing to lose.
An empty space where assurance used
to be
Now there's nothing but your own
confusion.

Jennifer Parkes (14)
King Edward VI School

MY BACKYARD SHED

My shed at the end of my yard has always lingered in the corner,
I've always seen it and wondered what was inside.

Could it be a hideout for the FBI,
or just a place in the corner of my eye?

Maybe it's not really there, or just a figure of my imagination,
but what if it is there - should I dare to enter,
should I dare?

I looked to see that the bolt was open,
what's the harm in a little peep?

The old wooden door opened with a creek,
as I opened it, eager to know what was inside.

I jump to find there's a person inside, a man leaning against the side,
he says and does nothing, as I hesitate to move closer.

Step by step I attempt to talk to him,
but all there was, was silence.
Is he dead?

The wind from the yard blows,
as I find it isn't a man at all, it's my dad's old work jacket
hanging on a peg on the wall.

Something rattles in the corner to catch my attention,
from the corner, scuttles a barn mouse from a paint pot.

It scatters away, leaving me shaking like a frightened animal
in the corner.

I leave the shed,
knowing never to be so nosey again.

Lisa Tippett (14)
King Edward VI School

YOUR SHOES

You made me go, I had no choice,
You ignored me, wouldn't listen to my voice
I can't come back after what was said
You probably wouldn't care if I was dead.
Life's so difficult, so unfair
You don't understand, you just don't care.
I'm out here freezing, hungry, cold.
You could try and understand me, you weren't always old.
You say you love me, you wish me well
Why do I feel you've put me through hell?
I didn't mean it, I want to come home
Help me Mum, I feel so alone.

Ciara Corrigan (14)
King Edward VI School

YOUR SHOES

My life is empty and hollow,
I have no one left to follow.
My head is filled with shame,
Please let this life begin again.
I need some time to think,
So please let me be alone.
I have nowhere else to go,
I feel so sad and low.
I will come back home,
Just give me time,
And I will make you see,
That time is all I need.

Sarah Byford (14)
King Edward VI School

GRIEF

Grief rips into you like a lion devours its prey.
It stalks,
And never leaves you;
Until finally you can turn away.

It tears at your heart,
Gripping you in its claws,
You'll never quite come apart.

Until gradually, so gradually,
The grief begins to fade.
But never again,
Can you think of that person;
Without feeling a loss and dismayed.

Rebecca Williams (15)
King Edward VI School

HARROD'S DOORWAY

It's not a lot, but it's my home.
I feel secure. I know I'm not safe.
An open space. But I'm enclosed -
Corners, cold, uncomfortable.
Damp and dark.
I am surrounded, with people, light.
But yet I am alone.
It's not a lot, but it's my home.

Camilla Wilcock (14)
King Edward VI School

ALONE

That fateful night,
Brought your feelings to light,
You never liked me,
You never loved me,
Dad called me a whore,
As I walked out the door.

I sit here all alone,
Thinking what I have done.
Will I survive?
Have I enough to stay alive?
You just sit there,
You don't even care.

If I came home,
Would you make me welcome?
Would you want me there?
Would you show me love and care?
I'm never coming back to you,
Whilst you treat me as you do.

Matt Howard (14)
King Edward VI School

WHAT WILL THEY GAIN?

All this anger, all this pain,
At the end of this, what will they gain?
All day long, they never stop,
Guns they shoot, and bombs they drop.
Walking around in the north of Ireland,
Frightened children, hand in hand.
The IRA - they don't care,
Trapping people, like in a snare.
Innocent victims afraid to come out,
Scared they'll be killed by an angry lout.
Living in danger, living in fear,
People forever crying, always shedding tears;
All this hurt, and for what reason?
It's never going to stop, from season to season.
Soldiers fighting in war after war,
Can't they see, it's becoming a bore?
They have no feelings, they can only hate,
There will be no more people left at this rate.
All this anger, all this pain,
At the end of this, what will they gain?

Rachel Blackburn (15)
King Edward VI School

TIME

A pendulum swings,
A number flashes,
The second hand spins,
But what is the time?

The sun rises and the sun sets,
Day and night,
Every day,
But what is the time?

Did time begin,
And will time end?
There may be a day
When time will freeze
And we will be frozen in time,
Trapped frozen in a universe no more.

A clock ticks on,
And keeps the time,
But is time real
Or just part of the 'imagination'?
How can a device keep the time,
For when did time begin,
And when will time end?

Gemma Willcox (14)
King Edward VI School

MILLENNIUM MADNESS

The government are building a Millennium Dome,
It will be made from plastic or chrome.
They will fill it with exciting stuff,
And as if all that is not enough -
You can even go and visit,
And pay so they make a profit.

The National Lottery are funding this project,
But why a dome? Where's the logic?
Why not a proper building to celebrate the millennium
Or something that will live on like a giant geranium?
There will be a huge human figure in the centre,
But they can't decide on its gender.

What would our ancestors think of this bid?
I'm sure they'd be horrified to hear what we did
And what about our children's future?
By then, the dome will be a shopping centre.
The people who made it possible were
Mandleson and Hessletine,
I suppose we should be thanking them -
All in good time!

Claire Burgess (15)
King Edward VI School

Progress: 20th Century Style

Computers replace people:
Shutdown begins.
Brains melt into microchips:
Feelings, intelligence binned.

Technology replaces industry:
People's jobs lost.
Friction occurs, tempers fray:
Harder to meet rising costs.

Sky TV replaces great outdoors:
Zombies are we.
Turn into mindless amoebas:
Remote in hand, forgetting trees.

Roads replace countryside:
Tarmac is laid.
'Look at the unspoilt cement.'
Earth becomes a darker shade.

Progress replaces life:
Improvements replace normality.
People become a small formality
That just get in the way.

Emma Hilder (15)
King Edward VI School

AWAKENING

He woke,
Into the darkness,
Unaware of his surroundings.
How long had he slept?
He reached for the bedside clock,
But his fingers met rough wood.
Puzzled he attempted to sit up.
His head bumped something hard.
Listening,
He heard nothing,
Or perhaps something,
Someone digging.
Why?
Was that the sound of rain falling,
Or small stones being dropped?
It seemed quite close.
Perhaps it was a dream,
But it seemed real enough.
He began to feel frightened.
But the shovels kept digging,
And the soil kept falling,
Onto the rough coffin lid.

Lindsay Johnson (14)
King Edward VI School

THE DEADLY POOL

He ran to the edge of the pool.
Running to the springboard,
He vaulted into the air; A perfect dive.
Too late, he smelt the fumes that were rising.
In another half second, he hit the surface and
dropped headfirst into the liquid.
It gripped him with paralysing brutality, from the
crown of his head to the soles of his feet.
His delicate skin felt everything.
First, a sudden scorching by ten thousand whips of
fire, each biting spitefully into his flesh.
Then, as he screamed, the acid began to torture him
to death,
Dissolving his hair, burning and blinding his eyes.
Accomplishing an unspeakable cruelty to his body,
It choked back his screams by pouring into his mouth.
There, it murdered the tastebuds and flowed down
his throat and lungs and into his stomach.
Every moment seemed to last a century, but it was
really a fairly quick death.
It was followed by a deep silence -
a silence in which the acid continued to eat his
corpse as it slid slowly into the depths.

Joanne Foyster (14)
King Edward VI School

A GRAVEYARD

The long winding stony path,
leads towards the crumbling tombstones
covered by creeping ivy,
that crawls up the nearby trees.
Their swaying branches,
cast eerie shadows on the cobbled ground below.
Like ghostly figures,
searching for their lost lives.
Through their tangled limbs
the pitch black sky is revealed,
stretching out into the unknown.
The sparkling stars form symbols
perhaps meaningful to another life.
Their long bony fingers seem to be reaching out,
beckoning you into their cold, dead world.
The fading names on tombstones,
wipes out their existence
from the world they once knew so well.
The gentle howling wind,
resembles the quiet sobbing spirits
trying desperately to find the life for which they long.

Liz Walden (14)
King Edward VI School

THE JOURNEY

When you are young,
Everyone is the same,
Everyone is equal.
As you grow older,
Divisions are built
Like a wall to keep people out.
Some find life easy,
And float along like a feather in the wind.
Others find it hard,
And tumble down like a rock down a jagged
                                        mountain.

She travelled down the easy road,
Overcoming everyone and everything,
And obstacles never appeared in her path.
Fate and luck were nestled over her head like a halo.
Success, triumph, wealth.
She had everything.

I took the hard road,
Tumbling down,
And slowly but surely climbing up again.
Fate and luck were swarming over my head like a black cloud.
Success,
Of overcoming obstacles
Wealth,
Of knowledge
But in the end I gained more.

Delaney Mabry (14)
King Edward VI School

TEA

Yorkshire is lovely,
Earl Grey is nice,
Darjeeling is cobblers, it's twice the price.

Drinking English tea is what I like,
I don't like coffee,
It's American tripe.

The thought of coffee makes me sick,
I'd rather have a cup of tea to lick.

The French drink coffee,
We drink tea,
That's why we beat them at Agincourt,
That's how it is to me.

The kettle was on when Nelson lost his eye,
Just off the Corsica shore,
'Never mind that' said Admiral Hood,
Shall I be mother and pour?
When I die they shall bury me,
With any luck in a crate of tea.

I'm fantastic and so are all my friends,
God save the Queen,
God save Sir Alec Guinness,
God save wonderful me,
God save lots of things but most of all save tea.

Kevin Johnson (14)
King Edward VI School

EX-DAUGHTER

My life became a constant fight,
between my wrong and their right.
I was angry and frustrated at their narrow minded views,
that should have stayed in the Stone Age.
The critical approach they brought to my every move,
meant I always had to lose.
So I took the easy way out and left,
I'm scared but powerful.
I'm unhappy that I had to, but both sides
can be happier now.

Sophie Lightfoot (14)
King Edward VI School

IS THIS A CASE FOR MULDER AND SCULLY?

Is this another case for Mulder and Scully?
Are the X-Files over yet?
Mulder is looking for the supernatural
Scully for scientific reasons but
They both face a world of uncertainty
Not being able to trust anyone
Even each other!

The weird, the unnatural
Investigations . . .
Searching for the truth
What's behind the *UFOs?*
All roads lead to the government
Tests on innocent people
Abduction who is responsible?
No one knows
But the *truth is out there* . . .

Sarah Winyard (14)
Leiston High School

WHY ME?

Years ago death was a fact
Had to happen, but know
These people think they can live forever
People are being frozen
Or put in suspended animation.

Before my job was easy.
I would just sail down
Grab some old geezer
while he was dreaming
Without any fuss, it was easy.

Now, not only are people getting frozen
There are new inventions
Double glazing, draft excluders
Which are really hard to get through
They give me back hell.

I mean,
What do these people
Want to live longer for?
You just have to put up with
all the pain again.

Oh, I'm getting too
Old for this game
Just think how many miles
I've done
I think it's time I retire.

Maybe my son Pestilence
Could take over
he needs a job
I can't bear thinking about it
No job for my boy.

Stuart Last (15)
Leiston High School

HER MAJESTY'S CREST

They have this sort of smartish uniform,
so you'd expect them to be reasonably bright,
but of course they're the easiest people to outwit,
if you're quick enough.

They have nothing better to do
but to stop little children, think of something
they might have done, and take their names.
'Name?' 'Charlie Sheen' 'Address?' '408 *ABBA* Road' 'DOB'
'25.12.94'

Speed bumps best describe what they do all day,
when they aren't waiting outside shops
expecting an old lady to do an armed robbery
whilst collecting her pension, with a banana.

Are they open when you need them most?
9am-12pm and 2pm-7pm, but if something happens
after these hours, then you'll just have to wait, won't you?
But nothing ever happens when they aren't open,
or so they must think.

If someone gets shot at 11pm then it'll have to wait till morning,
unless it's a Sunday then you'll have to wait till 9 o'clock Monday.

They never actually make proper arrests,
only on little children for stealing lollipops from their friends
or someone who's caught dropping litter in their own garden.

You hardly ever see them out of their cars
only to go to the shop for a packet of cigars (and a Lion Bar.)

If they had to deal with a proper crime,
would they know how to make an arrest?
(They could use the manual in their car called: 'How to make an arrest'
by PC Plod,)
and even then it would take them a day or two!

Do you feel safe knowing how efficient your local constabulary is?

Ben Peskett (15)
Leiston High School

ALL ALONE

Leaves on the trees rustle as I walk down this lonely path
Nothing can be heard for miles,
Apart from the wind whistling in the grass.
A figure moves, across the lane, staring right at me,
I know for certain it's not real,
I know what I should do but my brain doesn't function.
I start to *scream,* and run away,
I can feel its presence everywhere,
A terrifying 'hum' is coming over me,
'Hum! Hum! Hum! Hum! Hum! Hum!'
The wind, trees, grass all going 'Hum!'
I keep running till I meet a light,
But, still, nobody to be seen,
A dog barks, I jump!
I call out for help, but nothing,
I run and run till I get home.
Nobody believes me about what I saw
Perhaps they would if it happened to them!

Hayley Shimmon (14)
Leiston High School

ADOLESCENCE

Oh! To be eighteen,
When the world is your oyster,
When decisions are your own,
Instead of being made for you.

The worries, the fears at present,
The ups, the downs,
At times become too great, to think about,
Who you love or hate.

Wanting to do your own thing,
But being told that is wrong,
Excited about one thing,
Which seems trivial to another,

Want to be a child again,
With no 'hang-ups' or emotions.

Life is simple when you're young,
But then you hit your *teens*
Your friends are so important,
So why do they fall out?

Because of something silly,
Which nobody cares about,

What to wear to that disco?
What to have for tea?
It all seems so important,
But then, they are to me!

Tomorrow is another day,
so I must look forward,
To times when I am,
Past my teens as,
Life is a gift which,
Has been given to me.

Gemma Nuttall (15)
Leiston High School

GENERATIONS

Amidst the cold and immortal smell,
Stone figures are staring into the darkness of hell.
As I walk towards them trying to find
My ancestors from generations and generations behind.
I notice how they smile in their own conceited way,
And make the world stand still, as they laugh with dismay.
In the thick of the bushes, the graves are lifeless and still,
With their clammy moss and dank vegetation, they create an eerie chill.
As night and obscurity falls on this infernal region,
The whistling winds seem to control the trees' tormenting legion.
Owls squeal and scout as they catch their midnight feast,
And screech when they hear the footsteps of the beast.
Out of the trees and into the church, I see religious symbols on all walls.
I shiver as I am alone and imagine someone calls,
As I run and try to escape from the nightmare,
I try to remember a reason of why I went through with this dare.
The silhouette stands out,
And there is no doubt,
It is the scariest place,
And I'm proud to trace,
That I went there,
And went through with my dare!

Rebecca Ellis (14)
Leiston High School

BITE BACK

Endless fear and horror stories,
Kids pressed against the aquarium walls,
Men in cages, filming silently,
The smell of their fear drives me crazy.
Endless documentaries on:
'The Horrors Of The Deep',
And that stupid music to boot.
Not the best of lives,
I'm sure you'll agree.
Boats full of tourists,
Pointing and saying,
'So vicious!'
'Don't fall in, or he'll eat you!'
The amount of waste they put
In the sea each year, must warrant
A bite or two, mustn't it?
It's only fair to expect
Compensation.
I'm not evil, I'm just hungry.
Who'd be a shark?
If you're wild, you're a killer,
And if you're in captivity,
You're a plaything.
And they keep playing that stupid music . . .

Chris Pflaumer (15)
Leiston High School

THE LOSS OF THE TITANIC

The unsinkable ship has gone
although it did not last very long.
The rich jewellery which was once worn with pride
was also taken down on the terrifying ride.
The propellers will never turn
and the coals will never burn.
The grand staircase which stood so proud
is now covered by the sea's icy shroud.

The captain still haunts the deck
even though he went down with the wreck.
The terrible fright
occurred in the night.
As the iceberg loomed
the Titanic was doomed.
1,500 perished in the icy cold sea
some still clinging to the floating debris.

If anyone knew they were to collide
there would be no one taking this ride.
But no one could predict this fate
which was about to encounter this massive weight.
This was going to happen whether they liked it or not
they knew straight away it had sailed its last knot.

James Lapwood (13)
Leiston High School

MEN A NECESSARY EVIL

What is good about men?
Can't think of a thing
What is bad about men?
Just about everything!

Manly, magnificent, masculine - or so they think
When in reality some of them really stink
For they are vain, pompous, egotistical, and not really practical at all
It is us, we poor women, who bail them out
When on their backsides they fall.

They spend the housekeeping on beer and fags
And leave their wives to carry the shopping bags
this makes them look great in front of their mates, well, this is what
they think
'Look at me boys, I'm not under the thumb'
'Her place is by the sink!'

They rarely hold open a door for their wives
these bad manners come as no surprise
For being selfish, is one thing they really excel
Well, what else would you expect from a brainless brat?

Messily leaving their clothes in a heap
It's enough to make a poor woman weep
Lazing in front of the tele with a beer in their hand
Falling asleep, as their waists expand.

And when it comes to lend a hand, you might as well ask for the moon
For most men are bone idle and will not do a thing
Unless there's something in it for him!

So proud of a beer gut, that a rhinoceros would hate
He will say with great pride
'It's all paid for Mate.'

What a pathetic existence it must be for *men*
Thank God, I was born to be a woman - and not one of *them!*

Claire Edmed (15)
Leiston High School

WHERE DID IT GO?

The moon was full,
The wind was howling,
Suddenly there was a flash of lightning.
The window swung open,
A dark figure appeared.
I gasped in horror,
I jumped up at once,
And started to cry,
'Get out, get out!'
I turned on the light,
And saw its face.
Its glowing eyes looked right back at me,
I started to shake,
I thought I was doomed.
I turned on the light,
And then it was gone.
Where did it go?
Had I been dreaming?

James May (15)
Leiston High School

WORK

Why do we work?
Is it because we want to?
Is it to earn money?
Is it all worth it?
Why do we work?

Is it fair how some of us work?
9.00am to 5.00pm solid, with barely a stop - for so little
While others sit around doing nothing,
Getting bored but earning a fortune?
Why do we work?

Do we work to come home to an empty house?
And find ourselves sat in front of a TV?
Some people find this daily routine
for five days a week.
Yet, there are others out there,
earning a lot more
and going out enjoying their modern lifestyle
Why do we work?

Stuart Pegg (15)
Leiston High School

OBJECT

On a very cold night,
I see a very weird sight,
Flashing lights all around,
What object have I found?

The object is floating in the air,
This sight is very rare,
A beam seems to pull me in,
The aliens seemed very thin.

They tied me up with some rope,
In my heart there was some hope,
That I'll get out of this some day
And everything will be okay.

But then they pulled out a knife,
And I thought this is the end of my life,
They jabbed a needle I could not see,
I fear it is the end of me.

Lee Goddard (14)
Leiston High School

Doug!

Doug is in the wood,
He is playing Robin Hood.
Doug falls down a hole,
With a dirty mole.

Doug gets up,
He looks like a messy pup.
Doug is scared and runs,
He thinks there are guns.

Doug is in a room,
A gap in the roof shows the moon.
Doug sees a pale blue ghost,
It disappears and the room roasts.

Doug is burnt and dead.
He is now in his underground bed.

Daniel Mann (14)
Leiston High School

THE ENEMY

With my face pressed against the frozen ground,
I lie silent while the enemies surround.
As stamps of dreaded footsteps depart,
I see my brother with a bleeding heart.
I search for some others still alive,
but I am the only one to survive.

Severed bodies of friends enclose my eyes,
and out there the murderer pries.
Over the corpses, I noiselessly creep,
expecting someone to suddenly leap
out and knock me down from behind.
Thoughts of death won't leave my mind.

I drop down hard in an instant,
certain I'm dead, but the shots are distant.
The shivers shoot down my spine
and wind and trees together whine.
The noises play with my ears
as unknown to me the enemy nears.

I hear the footsteps back again
follow me slowly up the lane.
In fright my heart pounds
at such awful, deadly sounds.
As fast as my legs will take me,
I run into the shadows of darkest ebony.

He searches so close, but he can't find me,
hiding in scrub so thickly lined.
In anger he gives up his search,
I breathe again, no longer left in the lurch.
But the enemy will never go away
and helpless, all I can do is pray.

Elizabeth Smith (14)
Leiston High School

WHAT WAS IT?

In the dark
And lonely street,
I was to walk
But what to meet?

The sky was black,
And the air was cold,
If I was to live,
I had to be bold,

I saw the creature,
Standing there,
With smelly breath,
And spiky hair,

I looked and froze,
It seemed so scary,
At ten feet tall,
It was no fairy!

I realised then,
I had no chance,
There was no need,
For my advance,

So tall it stood,
But smiled with glee,
Before I knew it,
It squashed me!

Raymond Garlick (14)
Leiston High School

THE RHYTHM OF THE NIGHT . . .

Joy in the air,
On this uncalm night,
We played truth or dare,
It was late but still bright,
I needed help, I was trapped,
It began to feel tight,
Something or someone pulling,
Their body wrapping around mine.
It was my mate, of course.
We came to an entrance,
The entrance of a cemetery,
Then we chanted *'dare'*
We walked her in,
We all jumped.
We hit a bin of grit.
We *'dared'* her to uncover one of the bodies,
The freshest body,
Mrs Darling's grave.
We must have stepped over a body,
There was a steep bump,
Which Amy had tripped over,
Then, a quiet girl had *gone*.
Down into a dark empty hole.
We heard her bones hit the bottom,
All so sudden she was *gone*.
Why, why did we play that game?
I got all the blame,
Do not play that game - truth or dare!

Lisa Sillett (14)
Leiston High School

126

NIGHTMARE

A cold wet night
We were both soaked through.
All of a sudden,
Your eyes filled with horror,
You let out a piercing scream,
And you fell to the floor
Blood all up the shop window.
I rolled you over,
And put my head on your chest,
To hear your heartbeat,
Saying 'Goodbye, goodbye, goodbye,'
I felt your last breath on my neck,
I heard your last word,
I felt your last heartbeat,
Then nothing,
Except a cold wind.
I sat beside you,
Your face so pale,
Your blonde hair,
Red from your blood,
Then I left you to rest in peace,
That horrible night still haunts me,
I lie in bed and think,
I hope I never have to go through that again,
My first, but not last, nightmare.

Veronica Pearce (15)
Leiston High School

A Sea's Life

The rough sea,
The calm sea,
Whatever the sea,
It is the sea,

The sea is rough,
Rough is the sea,
It pours it roars it takes the sand away,
It tips it rips - you will surely stay away.
The sea is rough,
Rough is the sea.

The sea is calm,
Calm is the sea,
It sleeps, it weeps, it gently slips away,
It sways, it lays, it slowly finds its way.
The sea is calm,
Calm is the sea.

Joe Rennison (10)
St James CE Middle School, Bury St Edmunds

Fireworks

Damaging, crashing, trashing rockets
Clatter, pop and bang is what they sang
Hazardous, disobedient, wicked rockets
Bloody red and yellow in the sky
Orange and green, what a sickening colour
Enormous, colossal, gigantic rockets
What a sight I saw that night.

Kurt Smith (12)
St James CE Middle School, Bury St Edmunds

THE GHOST TRAIN

'Go on Mum please let me go'
'You'll have nightmares'
'No I won't'
'You'll get sick'
'No I won't'
'Okay then, here is 50p.'

I chose the seat right at the front,
Handed the man 50p,
And strapped my seat belt on.
I notice I'm the only one there
Except for a little girl
Who comes and sits next to me.

The ride starts, it all goes dark
I don't see any ghosts.
I say to the girl next to me
'Huh, this ain't scary.'
I spoke too soon as two glow-in-the-dark skeletons
Jumped out in front of us.
I screamed which was quite embarrassing
Because the little girl next to me
Just yelled out 'cool!' and gave me a funny look.
I stuck my tongue out at her
But there was no point because it got dark again.
I just closed my eyes
Whilst the other ghosts and devils
Suddenly jumped out at us.
The little girl said 'Don't be such a baby'
and pulled my hands away from my eyes.
Then the ride got faster and faster
I started to feel nauseous.
It went faster and faster and Burgh!
I walk dizzily back to my mum.

Althea Tester (12)
St James CE Middle School, Bury St Edmunds

LET'S CELEBRATE!

Birthday parties, birthday parties, aren't they just great,
Getting presents and cards I love the best,
But kisses from my Granny I hate!

Hallowe'en and Trick or Treating,
For some kids it's just like dreaming,
Dressing up is the best,
Giving candy is the worst,
But costumes could leave people screaming for a nurse!

Leaving school, leaving school, some think that's the best,
Because you get six weeks of nothing but fun and play.
But the people who enjoy it the most,
Are the teachers who get six weeks rest!

Christmas and the New Year, I think that's the best,
Because it is a time to share with others.
But when the tree goes down and Mum says 'Next year,'
That's what I detest!

Coming up to the Millennium soon,
I think that will be the bomb,
Probably never get to see it again,
Because old age will come!

Ashley James Browne (12)
St James CE Middle School, Bury St Edmunds

ELEPHANTS

Strong white tusks,
Big for the adults,
Small for the babies.
Long and hairy trunks,
All there is is grey and more grey.

Their feet are big,
With big toenails.
Their ears big and wobbly,
That's what I love,
About elephants.

Lizzie Gillard (12)
St James CE Middle School, Bury St Edmunds

GUY FAWKES

Oh my God it's huge
It's the largest ever seen,
It sparkles, crackles and
Goes *boom!*

Fireworks fly
They fly in the sky,
Faster than planes and birds.

It flies, it flies
High in the sky
Singeing birds and animals
Sometimes deadly.

When it's dud it comes
Flying down and
Everyone goes *Boo!*

Sparklers are cool,
To stick in a pool
and make lots of steam.

Ryan Theobald (12)
St James CE Middle School, Bury St Edmunds

SPA 1998

Red, green, go!
Good start from the Canadian
Bad start from Schumacher
That's Coulthard! He's hit the barrier
Irvine! Panis! Trulli! Oh dear!
Total wreckage,
They'll have to restart!

Here we go again!
Good start from Hill and he takes the lead
Hakkinen! Herbert! They're out of the race
Safety car - good choice!

Adrian Easton (12)
St James CE Middle School, Bury St Edmunds

A SOUND OF THUNDER

The past. So powerful yet so delicate to the touch of a
human hand or foot.
The path. Indestructible, but so easy to break the web of time.
The butterfly. So gentle, yet it changed the world and all
known happiness.
The dinosaur. Eyes like rolling eggs, teeth like daggers, and a
mouth set in a deathly grin.
The gun. Loud and terrifying, a sound of thunder.
Killing this giant monster, leaving it a stagnant heap on the
prehistoric ground.
Eckels. Dead! Killed by the terrifying sound of thunder.

Helen Sanderson (12)
St James CE Middle School, Bury St Edmunds

FIREWORK NIGHT

I see the fire burning bright,
it is as hot as a desert.
I see the stars and fireworks,
they're like a rainbow in the sky.
I see the wood burning bright with all its might
It tries to fight but slowly it burns away.

I watch the people standing there
watching the fireworks flare.
I watch Guy Fawkes being burned
for the sin he has earned.

Alex Reed (12)
St James CE Middle School, Bury St Edmunds

MY WORLD

I sometimes feel . . . so sad about my world.
It's a place where the environment is being destroyed with
graffitti, litter, pollution.
I remember . . . when our world was so clean and free from
pollution and how it's just destroyed.
It makes me think . . . that what we are doing to the environment like
the air, sea pollution, toxic waste.
But then I think . . . it can become a better place if everyone tries
their hardest.
Why can't I . . . stop all these terrible things happening to the world?
Perhaps . . . it will make people realise this is killing lots of people
and animals.

Donna Burlingham (12)
St James CE Middle School, Bury St Edmunds

STUCK IN A DREAM

I wish I could wake up in my own room
And hear the sound of breakfast being made.
The slamming of the cupboard door,
The banging of the fridge,
My mum knocking on my door,
With a cup of tea in her hand.
My step-dad saying:
'You always look pretty ugly in the mornings.'
And nagging me to tidy my room.
I miss my big sister shouting:
'Get out my room *now!*'
And my little sister shouting:
'Please can I have a go on the Nintendo?'

Holly Youles (12)
St James CE Middle School, Bury St Edmunds

FUNFAIR

We got to the funfair
The lights as bright as fire
I could hear people scream
Then I saw a high, high roller-coaster
Bright silver and red
People's hair rustling up in the air.
Then candyfloss, fluffy like a cloud high in the sky
A ghost train, green and blue.
We go through a tunnel dark as night
go whizzing round like a person on a bike
Then we had to go
'What time is the next fair Mum?
Please can we go?'

Laura Duchesne (12)
St James CE Middle School, Bury St Edmunds

A New Car

I'm speeding down the highway
In 2nd gear
Revving it up
White with fear.

I went too fast
My car is in bits
Now to repair it
Out come the tool kits.

I've got it back together
I used a pot of glue
Just a few scratches
It'll soon be good as new.

Lee Moye (11)
St James CE Middle School, Bury St Edmunds

Hallowe'en

Hallowe'en with ghosts and ghouls,
there's a monster in your swimming pool.
Trick or Treat, Trick or Treat,
there're vampires looking for fresh meat.
Witches, witches looking for you,
they want you for their brew.
You better watch out on that night
there's a monster waiting for a fright.
Hallowe'en it has been,
it was so frightening, it was a scream.

Sam Welsh (12)
St James CE Middle School, Bury St Edmunds

THE WORLD OUTSIDE

Newborn animals,
Sprouting their new life.
A long time later,
They die like a weed.

The sun is bright,
There is light all around.
The clouds come over,
No light to be found.

Brown leaves fall,
Scattered around.
People with rakes,
Scratching the ground . . .

A cold wind blows,
White cotton falls.
Scattered around me,
More cotton balls.

John Warren (12)
St James CE Middle School, Bury St Edmunds

MURDER IN THE DARK

Murder in the dark what a thought.
Especially if you got caught.
I wonder where you'd be?
In a dungeon with a thrown-away key.
But if you're lucky you'd still be in the woods,
But be careful!
There are traps on the ground.
And people watch you from around.

Willy Marsden (11)
St James CE Middle School, Bury St Edmunds

BONFIRE FUN

The fireworks were all blasting,
The Ferris wheels were swirling,
And the rockets were all blazing.

Some lovely food to much and crunch,
Burgers, hot dogs, and even swirly lollipops.

Everything was bright and shiny,
Things were whooshing, banging, blasting,
And blazing, everything was so loud.

There were sparklers, rides,
And even guys being burnt on bright bonfire,
Oh that was the best night I ever had!

Daisy Tayler (12)
St James CE Middle School, Bury St Edmunds

HALLOWE'EN NIGHT

On Hallowe'en night some stay in, some go out
and some do a whole different thing.

It's gloomy dark and lonely out there
for those who are lonely,
And it's spooky, dark and scary
for people who are a bit wary.

And there's people in costumes and masks
and they come up to your door and ask
'Trick or Treat?'

Danny Bowles (12)
St James CE Middle School, Bury St Edmunds

GUY FAWKES

On the 5th November,
When Guy Fawkes was burnt,
It is the time to remember,
But things must be learnt.

There's a firework display,
With lots of coloured lights,
You can remember this day,
On the darkest of nights.

Fireworks are fun,
But handle with care,
You must not run,
And you must beware.

As Guy Fawkes falls down,
We eat our chips,
On his face we see a frown,
And we smile and lick our lips.

Hannah Fensom (12)
St James CE Middle School, Bury St Edmunds

BODY PARTS

Tongues we use for talking,
Hands we use for clapping,
Feet we use for walking,
Knees are what we bend,
Mouths are meant for talking,
Then there's what we sit on.
And that's somewhere near the end!

Kelly Bryant (11)
St James CE Middle School, Bury St Edmunds

WHAT A GAME!

Hooray! Hooray!
What a day
Thetis is here today
Scowie and Johnno
are firing them in,
Making the fans sing
Here comes Dyer down the wing
What a cross!

Holland *goal!*

The fans sing -
1-0 to the football team 1-0
The away fans cry!
But the score won't change!

Phweep! There's the full-time whistle
And we're up in the Premiership!

Ashley Ruffles (12)
St James CE Middle School, Bury St Edmunds

FIREWORKS

Fireworks as silent,
As the wind
But as loud as a horn.
Bang! Crackle! Sizzle!
Whooshing past your ear
Faster than lightning
There it went, up, up, up.
There it goes
Quicker than life itself
Stop, it is no more.

Nicholas Hazelton (11)
St James CE Middle School, Bury St Edmunds

MY BROTHER

My brother is a big, big pain
He calls me names and teases
I shout at him in vain.

He tries to kick and punch me
I dart about the floor
I really think my brother is a gigantic bore.

He gets me into trouble
He blames it all on me
And on holiday he chases me
Into the cold blue sea.

His manners are appalling
He eats just like a pig
Although we tell him not to
He doesn't care a fig.

He never ever listens
To what I want to say
I think he's going to always
Be that way!

Emily Sim (9)
St James CE Middle School, Bury St Edmunds

THE SEAS

You hear the waves rumbling
Just as the waves are tumbling
It looks like a wonder
But it is really a terrible horrendous nightmare.

You see the waterfall falling
Making a splashing sound
You see sparkling water glisten
What a beautiful sight
So calm and quiet.

Daniel Hopkins (10)
St James CE Middle School, Bury St Edmunds

FANTASY FOOTBALL LEAGUE

Hello everyone I'm your commentator
For today's game we have perfect weather
And a great game in store too.

The first-half gets underway.
John plays a long ball to David.
David runs down the line.
Oh dear! He got tackled by the dustbin.
The dustbin runs around Josh who passes to the gutter.
The gutter passes it towards the bush,
But Jim intercepts it.
He runs and gets tackled by the grass.
Now it looks like Jim's in pain.
No! Wait a minute, he's up again.

John takes the free kick.
And it hits the tree,
Comes back out to David who shoots!
It hits the other tree,
Comes to Jim who hits it wide.

And into next-door's garden.
Sorry ladies and gentlemen
The game has had to be abandoned.

Daniel Whittaker (11)
St James CE Middle School, Bury St Edmunds

Rabbits and Sea Lions

It's so warm,
Warm is the sea.
Sea so quiet.
Quiet like rabbits.
It's so calm swaying,
Swaying side to side.
The quiet side of the sea.

Then suddenly a storm comes
It blows everyone away,
Except me.

The waves rushing,
It's roaring like lions,
Sea lions,
The sea lions raging,
Creeping up the shore,

Sea lions,
So angry,
What have I done?

Hollie Cogman (10)
St James CE Middle School, Bury St Edmunds

Grumpy Teachers!

Grumpy teachers, grumpy teachers,
They're the ones with small knobbly noses and wobbly knees.
Tiny, tiny feet as small as a mouse,
A mouse and a grumpy teacher don't mix,
Because soon she'll be screaming *h e l p!*
Will we help our poor darling teacher?
What do you think?

Laura Giles (12)
St James CE Middle School, Bury St Edmunds

THE STORM IN THE SEA

The fishermen go out at night
To pull the fish with all their might
The fish swim around horrified
But the fishermen don't care
They only have money on their mind
The sea is still again
You can hear the dolphins call
There's some people on the beach
Playing volleyball
Suddenly the sea starts to go grey
Then the tourists go away
The slash and clash, a storm has come
It spoils the whales' and dolphins' fun
The rain pours, the lightning flashes and increases its force
The clouds move in the wind to get to their course.

Tom Smith (9)
St James CE Middle School, Bury St Edmunds

IPSWICH TOWN FC

One night at Portman Road,
Adam Tanner made the blow.
The crowd shouted, 'Come on you Blues!'
But the others shouted 'Boo! Boo!'
Then the crowd shouted 'Hip, hip, hooray!'
As Keiron Dyer made the pass.
He took one step and put it in the net.
And by this time the goalie was very wet.

Alfie Startup (11)
St James CE Middle School, Bury St Edmunds

THINGS I'D DO IF IT WEREN'T FOR MY MUM

Go to school and muck around
Do cartwheels in the playground
Buy all the things I ever wanted
Make my mum think she's haunted
Paint my room violet and blue
Stuff my linen beside the loo
Call my gang the Charlie Girls
Always eat liquorice whirls
Usually hide from her
Let my mess occur
Always play
Go away
        Happily ever after.

Charlotte Colman (9)
St James CE Middle School, Bury St Edmunds

TEACHERS

Teachers fat, teachers thin
Teachers with a smiley grin.

Teachers shout, teachers talk
Teachers watch you like a hawk.

Teachers young, teachers old,
Teachers with a heart of gold.

Teachers ugly, teachers pretty,
Teachers that live in the city.

Chloe Symonds (11)
St James CE Middle School, Bury St Edmunds

ABC ALPHABET ANIMAL

Furry cuddly things
All shapes and sizes
Some big some small
Some f a t, some thin.

Furry, cuddly things
Colour is dim
Greys and dippy yellows
But then peacocks
Rose-red and river-blue and green

Furry, cuddly things
Furry, cuddly things.

Victoria Jones (11)
St James CE Middle School, Bury St Edmunds

MONSTERS ON THE MOON

Monsters from the moon come to earth
Crash, bash, flash, smash,
Bombs drop, monster to be shot
Crash, bash, flash, smash,
Foul, putrid, evil and sinister monsters
Bullets and grenades fly
Crash, bash, flash, smash,
Monster is shot, that ruined his plot.
Off he goes back to the moon
Crash, bash, flash, smash,
The war is over.

Charles Weston (11)
St James CE Middle School, Bury St Edmunds

ON YOUR OWN AT HOME

Live on lots of lovely food
Get in a big stroppy mood
Nick all the lovely money
Always be naughty and funny.

Watch the TV all day long
Make a big noise like a gong
Walk down the street have a fight
Watch rude programmes stay up all night.

Go to the Pizza Hut every day
Go on holiday to a hot bay
Eat big burgers and American chips
Chat up all the lovely chicks.

It would be cool without your mum
You could chew Wrigley's Orbit gum
Do what you want all day long
Don't have a bath and really pong.

And that's a poem without
Your mum.

Anthony Brown (10)
St James CE Middle School, Bury St Edmunds

ALONE IN THE JUNGLE

Alone in the jungle, cold and dark.
Dark night falls upon me
Me, alone in the jungle
Jungle lightens, the sun shining on me
Me, alone in the jungle.

Stephanie Jezard (10)
St James CE Middle School, Bury St Edmunds

THE SEA AND THE SUN

As the sun is found on the seabed
and rises out of its sleep.
It sees the sea down beneath him
and shines with all he is worth.
As the fish wake up they see the sun
and dance in the calm water.
The gentle sea shows her thanks
and ripples on the shore.

By noon the sea is angry
as the sun shines down on her.
She crashes and splashes against
the smooth rocks.
The little fish weave in the rocks
she grabs the fish and claws them out
and roars oh so loud.
'The sun and the sea are fighting again'
Said the wise old moon.
The moon is hiding where nobody knows,
Where nobody knows in the deep blue sea.

Rebecca Steed (10)
St James CE Middle School, Bury St Edmunds

THE SEA

In the sea
We play
In the night we sway
Going this way around me

On the beach
Sitting and put your hand in the sand
Lie in sand and dream.

Elliot Lees (10)
St James CE Middle School, Bury St Edmunds

IF I WAS RICH

If I was rich, I'd go down town,
I'd buy myself a golden crown.

I'd buy myself an entire house,
I'd buy myself a small, white mouse.

I'd wear the clothes I liked to,
I'd get a golden cherub too.

I'd visit the queen,
It would be such a scream.

I'd go to Spain,
I'd see Lois Lane.

I'd send Tony Blair,
Some spotty underwear.

Oh, I wish I was rich,
Don't you?

Amelia Sainsbury (10)
St James CE Middle School, Bury St Edmunds

THE WILD SEA

The wild sea,
Crashing on the rocks,
It's roaring, snoring, clashing,
It's angry, it's indestructible,
And the waves are strong,
The large waves run to you,
Running to the shore.

Kirsty Cross (10)
St James CE Middle School, Bury St Edmunds

LIFE WITHOUT MUM

Go shopping into town
Go on a roller-coaster upside down.
I really want to move house
What about the mouse?
In the garden all nice and big,
Take a shovel and dig, dig, dig.
Put the dolphin in the hole,
Oh no! He's eating my doll!
Pretend I'm swimming in the sea,
But don't forget my big TV!
Put my hair up really cool,
I really want a swimming pool.
I'll put my music on roaring loud, oh no!
I can see a big, black cloud.
But don't worry now, look come here,
I'll show you how!
Paint my room, just too bright,
Shut up you boys,' what a sight!
I'd buy a gigantic bed.
Go on, make sure I don't bump my head.
Oh no! Just look at my floor,
It's so messy,
What a bore!
No need to worry, just leave it to me,
I'll get it done, just you see!
No one to annoy me, no one to shout,
Hey! Do you know what I'm talking about?
Play computer games all the time,
Oh hooray sunshine.
Time to play,
Today is perfect . . .

Hooray!

Lucy Coogan (9)
St James CE Middle School, Bury St Edmunds

MY BROTHER

My little brother is mean
When he does something naughty
He'd rather not be seen!

He always annoys me
Even when he's good
He always destroys me
My mum said he could!

He *really* is a pest
He is very rude and
He never passed the test!

I have a book he likes
He always tries to get it
Then it turns into a fight
I said 'My brother would get it!'

My brother is six years old
Coming up to seven
I always thought he should be sold
Or have a holiday in Devon!

My little brother wants to stay
But there's not really much more to say!

Aziz Krich (9)
St James CE Middle School, Bury St Edmunds

THE TROUBLE WITH MY BROTHER

My brother is very annoying,
He thinks he's boss,
He gets me cross,
And then he leaves me toiling!

My brother always annoys me,
For when I was getting changed,
He burst into my room and put it in gloom,
And made me get stung by a bee!

Megan Williams (9)
St James CE Middle School, Bury St Edmunds

THE TROUBLE WITH MY BROTHER

He stinks the room out
So then I shout
'Get out of here!'
So I deafen his ear
'Ooohhh!' He goes
Then I stamp on his toes.

Once I played hockey
He suggested to be a jockey
I hate that
He said I was a bat
Then we finished our game of hockey.

It's great to be brothers
Although we can be
Nutters!
At the end of the day
Whether we fight or play
We always know come rain or snow
It's great to be
Brothers.

Alex Meyers-Bickel (9)
St James CE Middle School, Bury St Edmunds

BEES!

Why is a garden green and bright?
Why is a flower so delicately light?
Why in the summer do trees have leaves?
But then in the winter they're just like bees
Hiding away day or night.
Nothing could give them some sort of fright
They must be cold, they must be sad
Just like little angels, not ever bad,
Apart from stinging you it isn't their fault
They think you're just about to bolt,
Hating flowers, having power
They only want you to like honey
Not to eat a poor little bunny.
Stick up for them, make them happy,
There you go - you've got a friend!

Ruth Brooks (9)
St James CE Middle School, Bury St Edmunds

ROUGH SEA

The waves crashing on the shore
Sends the children running back,
Green and blue waves,
Some waves big,
Some waves small!

The waves crashing on the rocks,
They're tumbling
The sea is angry once again,
Children dive in and out of the waves
Some jump on them.

Amie Grimwood (10)
St James CE Middle School, Bury St Edmunds

THINGS I'D DO IF IT WEREN'T FOR MY MUM

Play with my friends,
for long weekends.
Only wash when the house
gets smelly,
put my feet on the table
and watch lots of telly.
Go to Disneyland every year,
drink lots and lots of
ginger beer.
Get a cleaner in every day,
have a party, shout hooray!
Never ever go to school,
stay at home in my swimming
pool.
Go to bed really late,
stuff myself with chocolate
cake.

Rachel Frost (9)
St James CE Middle School, Bury St Edmunds

THE MOTHER-LIKE SEA

The sea is like a mother, angry nearly always.
Snuffling and roaring as she goes.
Clashing and bashing, whooshing and pushing.

But sometimes she is gentle, soft, sleepy.
She just sits in a chair
Watching children play in the park
As she gets old.

Lee Freeman (10)
St James CE Middle School, Bury St Edmunds

THE ROUGH SEA

The rough sea with the rolling waves
It crashes at the rocks
It smashes at the boats
It is raging and angry,
It smashes at the rocks.
When the tide comes in people run from the danger,
But now it is gentle and calm, it is sleepy and smooth,
The sun shines on the sea and then it roars so loud
when the moon comes up into the black sky.

Sam Ponder (10)
St James CE Middle School, Bury St Edmunds

THE CALM AND SWAYING SEA

The sea is soft, soft as can be
The sea is gentle and silent and swaying
The sea is still
Still for me to dance and play
In that calm and swaying sea.

Alexandra Tayler (10)
St James CE Middle School, Bury St Edmunds

THE SEA

The rough sea crashing, smashing against the rocks.
You can hear it roaring against the cliff,
It's slowly lashing and wearing away at the rocks.

The quiet sea is smooth and gentle against the rocks,
It hits the rocks so silently you can't hear it,
Splashing and swaying on the beach so softly.

Andreas Fantousi (10)
St James CE Middle School, Bury St Edmunds

THE TROUBLE WITH MY SISTER

My sister spoils my games,
My sister calls me names.
She even did all this,
When we were on the Thames.

My sister annoys me when friends come,
My sister stops my fun.
Sometimes I wish I could stick,
Ants down her bum.

My sister likes to fight,
My sister turns off the light,
And she goes to bed,
Late at night.

Conal Dougan (9)
St James CE Middle School, Bury St Edmunds

ROUGH SEA

The waves crashing on the shore,
Waves rolling round and round
Children scared, run away
Loud smashings come
Whooshing past.

The waves lashing past me,
Splashing on the rocks, whooshing.
They're jumping over and over me,
Dolphins screeching and jumping around,
Green and blue waves
Splashing angrily.

Claire Fellingham (10)
St James CE Middle School, Bury St Edmunds

THE ROUGH AND QUIET SEA

The sea so quiet and gentle,
That when you put your hand in the water,
The sea strokes your hand,
So gently that you drift into a wonderful sleep.
You start snoring,
Then you wake up with a start,
The sea is roaring splashing clashing,
Then a stroke of lightning,
Then an indestructible wave,
Then bang!
Everything is quiet again,
The sea is lapping on the shore,
Like nothing has happened before.

Charlotte Dasan (10)
St James CE Middle School, Bury St Edmunds

THE SEA FOX AND HIS PREY

The sea is a fox prowling
Soft, slow and quiet.
Low and no movement . . .
. . . As it sees its prey.

Suddenly it leaps and rolls
Dashing and smashing its victim
Angry and daring
Indestructible is the sea

It goes quiet and slowly rolls away
Waiting, waiting, waiting
For its next time hunting.

Chloe Wiseman (10)
St James CE Middle School, Bury St Edmunds

MR SEA'S LIFE

Another day begins,
Rumbling, tumbling through the stones,
A spot of water hit my nose.

As night falls the sea creeps out of bed,
Causing mayhem wanting to be fed,
It thrashes the houses and beats the huts,
Everyone ends up with bruises and cuts.

It's quiet today,
The sea has not been out to play,
From then on the day stood still,
Silence, silence, pure silence.

Nothing is the same without the sea,
It was the companion embedded in me,
One day, the sea will return,
Willing to carry on life.

Nina Williams (10)
St James CE Middle School, Bury St Edmunds

THE SEA IS ANIMALS

The sea is like a fish when it's quiet.
Swaying in the sun and every time you catch a fish
The sea looses a calm wave.

The thunder comes, the sea turns into a crocodile
It's roaring, splashing, incredible.

But then the sky turns into a rainbow.
The sea is half crocodile, half fish.
Makes the shore a whooshing mess.

Jessica Ruddock (10)
St James CE Middle School, Bury St Edmunds

MY FIRST DAY AT SCHOOL

The morning came.
The big red school came closer.
I have been told all those that enter will pay!

I stepped quietly into the playground, where I saw my friends.
The whistle sounded horrifying as it screeched.
We all lined up then I saw a teacher, a fierce teacher!
As she came her every footstep was heart thumping.
Everywhere went quiet.

She led us in like beasts, towards the school.
I opened the door with a screech and walked to the top.
The staircase creaked as we walked anxiously to our classrooms.
We took off our coats and bags and hung them on the peg.
We walked silently in and sat on a seat - they creaked.
Then the teacher slammed the door and we all went silent!

Lucy Wallace (9)
St James CE Middle School, Bury St Edmunds

THE SEA

The sea like a beast roaring
Loud as a bomb booming
Lashing out at people near it
Angrily growling all night.

But in the morning it's quietly snoring
No longer is it angrily snarling
Slowly lapping on the beach
Children will happily play
On this calm sunny day.

Owen Jones (11)
St James CE Middle School, Bury St Edmunds

MY WEIRDEST DAY

Yesterday was really weird,
When I woke up I heard Mum sneer,
'Get up, idle lazy head!'
So I heaved my bones out of bed.
As I started to feed my cyberpet,
'I need to go to the supermarket!'
So I flung my pyjamas on the floor,
And took some day-clothes out of the drawer.
I went downstairs and ate my breakfast quick
I ate so fast I was nearly sick!
So we drove to the superstore and parked the car,
I ran to the entrance and left Mum far.
I gasped as I got inside the door,
Because of the weird sight I saw!
There was a cage of chimps in the corner of the room
And then suddenly with a loud *boom,*
They all woke up after being asleep,
Then I heard our car alarm beep,
But I crashed into a crowd of people chanting 'Chimp'
They knocked me over, I banged my leg and started to limp.
I told my mum and then I had to go to school,
And after doing swimming in the swimming pool,
I looked out of the window and there were lots of cats!
Lots and lots of them were thin but two of them were fat.
Lots of weird things happened when I was at school
So many it was as large as the swimming pool!
But now I've forgotten about the weird day
It seems so stupid anyway.

Tom Low (9)
St James CE Middle School, Bury St Edmunds

SPIRIT OF THE SEA

In the morning when the sun beams down,
I close my eyes tight, squint then frown.
I can't see because of the light but I can hear,
The lapping waves,
The lapping waves which are near,
The lashing, rolling, whispering waves,
Whispering waves,
I can hear it 'Get up and watch me' it says.
Ripples roll and touch my feet,
I feel the cold but I feel the heat.
As it surfs its own sky high wave,
The mood changes and turns into rage.
Twisters which are down, down deep,
Further than my feet can reach.
The waves fly,
The waves fly up,
And fill my hammock like a watery cup.
As the water drains like a sieve,
Through the holes of my hammock again to live.
Again,
Again,
Again the waves die down,
So now I can watch the sea,
By sitting and looking around.

Laura Rayment (10)
St James CE Middle School, Bury St Edmunds

THE MIGHTY DEEP

The sea is washing the sand away,
Taking every little bit.
Splashing against what were the still rocks,
The rough sea is banging,
The flag is booming.

The calm sea gently adrift,
Floating with no waves in sight.
The fish blowing bubbles,
Waves still, quiet.
The flag is fluttering.

Mark Nunn (10)
St James CE Middle School, Bury St Edmunds

MY LITTLE COUSIN

My little cousin drives me insane,
I could do without,
She's a real big pain.

I could do anything,
Even go to the moon,
But mum would call
'Come back soon.'

Every time she comes,
She has pop,
But guess who ends up getting the mop?

My little cousin,
She is quite fun,
But we always end up fighting,
When the day is done.

My little cousin drives me insane,
I could do without,
She's a real big pain.

Katy Jones (9)
St James CE Middle School, Bury St Edmunds

THE TROUBLE WITH MY SISTER

I think my sister is horrible,
I think my sister is strange,
But the thing that drives me round the bend
Is when she calls me names.

She kicks around the football,
She spoils all my games,
But the thing that makes me really mad
Is when I get the blame.

But the thing about my sister
When all is said and done,
Although I hate to say it
We have a lot of fun!

Jamie Ogilby (10)
St James CE Middle School, Bury St Edmunds

THE MIGHTY DEEP

The mighty deep is crashing up against the rocks.
The sea is roaring.
There is a tidal wave coming.
There are stones flying up from the bottom.
The white waves glance into the air and crash to the floor.
By noon the sea has calmed down.
The waves are very gentle and calm.
The sea is all green and blue.
The sandy shores are full of stones because of that storm.
The fish swimming come to the surface and blow bubbles.
The sun comes up from the horizon and the sea is calm and
the sun sets in the sky.

Ben Clements (10)
St James CE Middle School, Bury St Edmunds

BOYS

Here's the guide to attracting boys
For a start don't play with girlie toys
Comb your hair, put it in wacky styles
Put perfume on that you can smell for miles.

Wear short skirts, show off your legs
The best looking boys go to Kegs
Be as tough as you can
And as strong as a man

Go to gym, learn some tricky things
And don't forget, make sure you can sing
Dye your hair your favourite colour
Have some beer with your supper

Be very careful who you pick
And don't eat too much or you'll be sick
Pick a boy that's very good looking
Round your little finger - then you've got him.

Samantha French (9)
St James CE Middle School, Bury St Edmunds

THE UNWANTED BEACH

The calm sea silently comes back and forth
on the sunny beach.
The sea is sleepy and unwanted.
But when it comes to half-past three,
The rough sea comes rushing, rolling, crashing,
rumbling indestructibly,
Onto the gentle sunny beach.

Emma Brown (10)
St James CE Middle School, Bury St Edmunds

MY COUSIN

My cousin is taller than me,
She's big and bold,
But really she does not scare me.
She's just a kind giant to me.
Her smile on her face shines like the sun,
I treasure her like gold.
When she stops smiling the sun goes down
I beg her to smile again,
But it's the end of a long day.
The sun has to go down and the moon takes its place.
I can remember her even in my dreams.
She's stuck in my head, I can't get her out.
My cousin is lovely,
My cousin is my best friend.

Keira Whewall (9)
St James CE Middle School, Bury St Edmunds

THE SEA

The waves are green and blue
They roar all day,
Crashing and smashing on the rocks.

They rise up like a great wall of water.
By noon the sea is soft and gentle lapping up the stones.

But at night it grows loud
Again lashing out at people
And wrecking ships who cross its path.

Jake Juszkiewicz (10)
St James CE Middle School, Bury St Edmunds

STORMY SEA

The waves are crashing against the rocks,
there are ripples in the rock pools.
Crabs and creatures are searching for shelter,
and thunder filled the air.

After the thunder left the air,
lightning struck the shore.
Bright flashes light up the sky,
as the clouds drift away.

The sun has appeared,
shining and bright.
The sand has turned white,
and the day has turned hot.

Jennifer Allison (10)
St James CE Middle School, Bury St Edmunds

WHAT I WOULD DO IF IT WASN'T FOR MY MUM

Never wear any shoes in the house,
Stop having to be as quiet as a mouse,
Lean out of the window whenever I feel,
Have baked beans for every meal,
Dress my kittens in old dolls' clothes
So that you can only see their toes,
Sneak out at night and climb on the roof,
Listen to loud music with my friend Ruth,
I argue with Alice and never stop,
And risk nicking things from a shop,
I really think I have to stop,
Mum's chasing me with a mop.

Eloise Burnett (9)
St James CE Middle School, Bury St Edmunds

BEACH TIME

Umbrellas up,
shoes put down,
put on your cozzie,
run around
Splash!

Sun cream on,
jewellery off,
run to the water,
then go
Splash!

I love beach time!

Laura Thacker (9)
St James CE Middle School, Bury St Edmunds

BUBBLES

Blow
Bubbles
Watch them grow
Gliding, swirling
Like a shimmering
Rainbow slowly
Down they go
Away
Pop.

Alex Hart (9)
St James CE Middle School, Bury St Edmunds

AUTUMN FUN

There is a squirrel,
eating some nuts,
there are some conkers,
falling on ducks.

Autumn leaves fly,
in the morning sky,
orange and red,
soft as a bed.

There's a soft breeze,
it's making me sneeze,
there are ducks in a pool,
and the weather's quite cool . . .

Kevin Rutherford (10)
St James CE Middle School, Bury St Edmunds

WHAT I'D DO IF MY MUM WENT ON HOLIDAY

It would be brill to be me
I could go out, be free
I'd watch the telly all day long
I wouldn't even sing a song
I'd do what I like with my hair
Do what I want, even swear
I would invite round one of my friends
And of course the fun would never end.
Yes I would get in a mood
Of course I'd even eat junk food.

Joe Symonds (10)
St James CE Middle School, Bury St Edmunds

THINGS I'D DO IF IT WEREN'T FOR MY MUM

Put the tele on all day,
Play Nintendo 64 in any way
Get a rocket to outer space,
Turn myself into a superman that's ace,
Live on sweets, cake and milk,
Throw away any silk,
Ride my bike every day,
Mess up my room and always play,
Never ever go to school,
Spend my time playing pool.

Get my savings in my hand
Get a plane to Disneyland.

Alex O'Neill (10)
St James CE Middle School, Bury St Edmunds

THINGS I'D DO IF IT WEREN'T FOR MY MUM

Have a cleaner for the house,
Buy myself a pet mouse.
Have a holiday every year,
Buy my friends a souvenir.
Play the lottery,
Smash all the pottery.
Eat lots of chocolate,
Go to bed very late.
Never ever go to school,
Watch loads of football.
Never ever eat all my greens,
Always eat baked beans.

Laura Dowsing (9)
St James CE Middle School, Bury St Edmunds

DYSLEXIA STRIKES

Dyslexia is only just a word
I know what I want to say
but it comes out blurred.

I look at you
and I look at me
What is the difference?
I can't see.

Dyslexia means that I can't spell,
I can't read and I can't write.
It means all my life I'll have to fight
the constant battle that life invites.

Mark Ayre (9)
St James CE Middle School, Bury St Edmunds

WHAT I'D DO IF MY MUM WENT TO SPAIN

I could do things to my hair
And dance around, even swear
I could bring round one of my friends
Then the fun would never end
I could stink the house whenever I liked
And drink from cans all night
I could always eat junk food
I can even get in a mood
It would be brill to be me
I could go out and be free.

Ben Smith (9)
St James CE Middle School, Bury St Edmunds

LAST NIGHT

I ate burgers, hot dogs and ham
I drank Coke from a great big can
I've got a cat called Smokey Poos
He didn't like me because of my shoes
My shoes are smelly they really stink
Last night my feet went bright bright pink
My auntie Pam said she was coming
Round to our house to do some plumbing
Because our bath leaked last night
After Mum and my brother had a big fight.

Alice Lale (9)
St James CE Middle School, Bury St Edmunds

AUTUMN

All the leaves turn crisp and brown
Then fall softly on the ground
When all the leaves have fallen off
The tree lays bare with scrawny sharp jagged empty branches
Now all the leaves turn golden brown
Then *crunch, crunch, crunch!*
Footsteps come and destroy the leaves
The bugs and animals slither away
Worms dig through the ground
Then at last the crisp leaves disappear.

James Fenner (11)
St James CE Middle School, Bury St Edmunds

THE TIDE

The tide is coming in so quick
It will be up to my knees in a tick
It charges up the shore
Like a cheetah on all fours
As it scrambles over shingle
With golden sand it starts to mingle.

As the tide is going out
Children start to run about
The waves all gather into one
And glisten in the gleaming sun
People paddle in the sea
What a pleasant place to be.

Andrew Copsey (10)
St James CE Middle School, Bury St Edmunds

SOULFUL SOUNDS OF JOY

The soft creaking of the hammock,
Soft, soulful sounds.
The meek and docile ripples,
Roll along the scintillating sea.
Rays of light beam down on the turquoise water,
Making the whispering waves glow with radiance.
The sun sets and the sky floods with colour.
Warm air surrounds everything,
And wraps the area in a blanket of darkness.
Silence.
Silence.

Jennifer Evans (10)
St James CE Middle School, Bury St Edmunds

THE SEA

White horses, trotting
nearer and nearer
Crashing against the cliff tops
the waves rippling

The neighing echo of the sea
made me shiver
The swelling waves
drenched me

The horses started neighing wildly
it shook me up
They trotted up to me
then went back to the sea

The noise died down
You can hear the horse's hooves
and every single word
the sea sang.

Vicky Cawthorne (10)
St James CE Middle School, Bury St Edmunds

WAVES

The waves bellowed as they pounded in.
Ripple of waves between the mighty tempestuous waves.
The soft white sheen as they crash upon the sand.

Night draws in and the ripple of the waves
Soothes you to sleep.
Day, night the tide goes in and out.

Hannah Brookman (10)
St James CE Middle School, Bury St Edmunds

As I Looked Out To Sea

As I looked out o'er the ocean
All I saw was endless blue
Not a soul could I see out there
Just maybe a fin or two

As I listened to the ocean
All I heard was a swish and splash
Not a voice could I hear out there
Just maybe a quiet thrash

As I smelt the salty water
All I smelt was musky salt
Not a flo'er could I smell out there
Just maybe a salty vault

As I bent down to feel the water
All I felt was water cold
Not a tad of heat was in there
Just maybe a fish so bold.

Ian Walker (10)
St James CE Middle School, Bury St Edmunds

The Tranquil Sea

A wavelet hit the sand,
Now more waves are following, crashing against the cliffs,
A dolphin jumped up and broke it in two,
The waves tingled against the stones,
The cold, rushing waves hitting each other
Like white horses galloping around.
        Then silence . . .
The lapping of wavelets hitting the sand.

Alistair Palfrey (10)
St James CE Middle School, Bury St Edmunds

BROTHERS

My brothers are naughty
my brothers are sick
they think they're really clever
but really they're thick.

My brothers are ugly
my brothers are grim
my brothers are silly and
my brothers are dim.

My brothers are naughty
my brothers are sick
they think they're really clever
but really they're thick.

My brothers are drinkers
they go to the pub
they have a little shandy
and leave for the club.

My brothers are naughty
my brothers are sick
they think they're really clever
but really they're thick.

Joseph Barnet-Lamb (10)
St James CE Middle School, Bury St Edmunds

THE GREAT SEA STORM

The sea is calm when the tide is out, the waves are very slow.
But when the tide is coming in, the waves start to flow.
The waves get bigger and at the sand they gnaw.
The clouds get black and the rain starts to pour.

The waves start to turn and toss as the sea is getting rough.
But those people in sailing boats are finding it rather tough.
The storm seems to go on forever but finally starts to fade.
But the sea does not realise the damage it has made.

Kara Gates (11)
St James CE Middle School, Bury St Edmunds

MY BROTHER

My brother's called Paul,
and he's ever so small,
but he's only sixteen months old.
He's got green eyes and red hair,
he doesn't look like me at all.

My brother is a pest,
and I never get any rest,
when I look after him.
He's fun to play with even though
he wrecks everything I make.

My brother has the patience of a fish,
and he never keeps his food in a dish,
when I feed him he is messy.
When he walks into a wall,
he's got no sense at all,
he just rubs his head and walks away.

My brother's learning to speak,
he said 'Brother' only last week.
My brother's always on the go,
he likes to swim, run and climb.
I wish I could get some sleep!

Jack Anders (9)
St James CE Middle School, Bury St Edmunds

EXCUSES

Have you got your homework to hand in?
James, why did your mum put it in the bin?
Katie, even if your dog chewed your book,
You've got to learn, now look.
Sam leaving your back pack on the bus
Is not good enough, what a fuss.
Sarah, I know you forgot to take your work home,
It makes me cross, I just have to moan.
George, this sheet is a mess, did you write it in the bath?
Take that grin off your face, don't laugh.

Daniel J Price (9)
St James CE Middle School, Bury St Edmunds

AUTUMN

The colour of leaves turns from green to brown
Yellows and oranges too.
The leaves all fall off the trees
And float down to earth.
We jump in and out of the leaves
And have a great time.
Crunch, crackle, rustle, pop,
I wish autumn would never stop.

Steven Copsey (10)
St James CE Middle School, Bury St Edmunds

MY BROTHER

My brother is a bad bully
beats me up every day
and every night he scares me
I wish he'd go away.

My brother is a pain
every night and day
he wakes me up at 5 o'clock
and when I get angry
I could chase him round the block.

Sam Ratcliffe (9)
St James CE Middle School, Bury St Edmunds

WAVES

The waves are soft when they touch the land
They jump up to reach the golden sand
I go as close as I can get
And I jump back again or I'll get wet
I look for shells on the beach
'Look, there's a big one I cannot reach'
The sea is blue, green or grey
Depending on the type of day.

Agnes Tester (10)
St James CE Middle School, Bury St Edmunds

FOOD

I like chips, I like fish,
I don't like sprouts on a dish,
I don't like peas, I don't like carrots,
They make me think of yelling parrots,
I don't like custard, I don't like mustard,
If I'm forced to eat these I'll get flustered.
I like chips, I like fish,
I don't like broccoli on a dish.

Tyler Smart (9)
St James CE Middle School, Bury St Edmunds

STARS

Stars so cool
Stars so bright
they shine in the
night and it looks
really bright.

Stars are bright
in the night they
shine on the world
and at night the
world is shining
and bright from those
magnificent stars.

Lewis Kemp (9)
St James CE Middle School, Bury St Edmunds

THE SEA

The sea is like a road through life,
Rough, tough and calm,
Screaming, crying and sighing.

In the wacky woods above, the sea is as calm as a dove,
A drop of water on my nose that shows,
You might find that one day you're in luck,
Someone might find you who knows.

It's lonely on the island especially on your own,
The moon is like a sapphire,
Glowing in the night sky.

Hannah Hooper (10)
St James CE Middle School, Bury St Edmunds

BUBBLES

Bulge
sphere
hovering
huge small blue
multicoloured
exploding
transforming
gone.

Nicola Harris (9)
St James CE Middle School, Bury St Edmunds

THE BUBBLE

Float
Silvery
Transparent
Lightly   Sailing
Multicolour   Rainbow
Sparkly   Swirling
Fragile   Flow
Swirl   Down
Pop!

Jenny Tant (10)
St James CE Middle School, Bury St Edmunds

THE BUBBLE

Blow
Float, flow
Swirly, bright
Sparkle, opal
Shimmering, rainbow
Sailing, pink, pearl
Light, gliding
Going
Gone.

Rachel Johns (9)
St James CE Middle School, Bury St Edmunds

BUBBLE POEM

Blow
Drifting
Delicate
Wiggly, wee we
Multi-rainbow, whoosh
See-through, gliding
Transparent
Pop!

Steven Charles Long (9)
St James CE Middle School, Bury St Edmunds

BUBBLE

Blow
gliding
oil, purple
multicolour
shimmering, sparkle
bulbous rainbow
delicate
weaker
pop!

James Curtis (9)
St James CE Middle School, Bury St Edmunds

THE BUBBLE

Clear
Floating
Drifting fast
Changing its shape
Swirling, whirling, float
Gliding, shimmering
Oval transparent
Growing
Pop!

David Hanson (9)
St James CE Middle School, Bury St Edmunds

BUBBLES

floats
growing
in the air
swirling, sparkles
glitters and shines
wiggly, transforming
swirling in
a dream
pop!

Rebecca Cordell (9)
St James CE Middle School, Bury St Edmunds

THE BUBBLE

Light
Moving
Oval size
Bouncing away
Transparent, foamy
Growing, drifting
Wobbling
Twisting
Pop!

Amy Nicholls (9)
St James CE Middle School, Bury St Edmunds

BUBBLES

Float
Upwards
Wind blowing
Slightly drifting
Glistening bubble
Falling downwards
Wind pushes
Fading
Pop!

Harriet Smith (9)
St James CE Middle School, Bury St Edmunds

A SYLLABLE POEM - THE BUBBLE

Slow
Bubbles
Swirling quick
Rainbows whirling
Glittering spirals
Delicate sphere
Silvery
Fading
Pop.

Laura Webb (9)
St James CE Middle School, Bury St Edmunds

My Sister

My sister embarrassed me
when we were in the car,
we always get bored
when we go really far.

So we play games
like guess the colour of the car behind,
so we turn around and see
what we can find.

Sam turned around and waved,
the driver waved back,
so I hid behind my seat
and covered myself over with a sheet.

Although I felt embarrassed
I still love my sister
and if she wasn't there
I guess I'd really miss her.

Victoria Watts (9)
St James CE Middle School, Bury St Edmunds

School!

School school it's so cool
The teachers are nice
but the kids rule.
We run down the corridor
feet smacking on the floor
yesterday my friend, Steve ran into a door.

Adam Parker (10)
St James CE Middle School, Bury St Edmunds

PIKING LIGHTNING

Fast as a dash
quick as a flash
Then *snap!*
Another fish gone
It glides through the lake
Very opaque, a master of silence
a master of disguise
a master of *doom!*

Stuart James Farrell (10)
St James CE Middle School, Bury St Edmunds

SEASONS

Summer is a nice season
to have a party.
Spring is a hot season
to have an ice lolly.
Autumn is a cold season
to go somewhere warm.
Winter is a fun season
to play with your friends.

Katie Morgan (9)
St James CE Middle School, Bury St Edmunds

I DON'T WANT THAT AND DO WANT THIS

I want a kiss and not a new sis
My dad is sad 'cause he wants a new lad.
My mum likes football when she has a miss
The crowd goes *hiss hiss.*
Sometimes I'm bad because I go really mad.

James Starling (9)
St James CE Middle School, Bury St Edmunds

BECAUSE I'M FAT AND UGLY

Because I'm fat and ugly
I wish I had a friend.
People just walk by me
They don't want to know me.
I get very lonely
Even my dog turns his nose up at me.
I look up into the sky
I wish I had a friend.
But one day I was alone
Fiddling with stones.
A new girl came up to me
And we talked and we played
Now I know that girl and
She taught me something.
It doesn't matter what you look like
And how heavy you are,
That girl's name is Emily,
She introduced me to Alice
And now we're the terrible threesome
And we're all best friends.

Jade Woodward (9)
St James CE Middle School, Bury St Edmunds

THE MAN FROM FRANCE

There was a man from France
Who learnt the boogie dance
He danced all night and he danced all day
He was having so much fun he got carried away
He felt so happy he started to pray
And said 'Dear God can I do this every day?'

Stuart Dixey (10)
St James CE Middle School, Bury St Edmunds

MY DAD

My dad is great
He's my best mate
He is really funny
and gives me pocket money
He is special to me
as you can see
He is football mad
He's my super dad.

Lauren Evans (9)
St James CE Middle School, Bury St Edmunds

MY BIRTHDAY

My birthday's in December if I can remember,
It's near Christmas, I share it with my twin sister
Which is fun but that means I don't get much cake.
I don't care because I share my birthday with
Someone loving and caring like my sister.
But I wish I had my own birthday
But for heaven's sake it's not too late
I'll just have it next year in November.

Megan Evans (9)
St James CE Middle School, Bury St Edmunds

PLEASE LISTEN BECAUSE I'M BLIND

I can't see like others do
I can't read or write
Why am I so unlike you?
Because I have no sight.

I'd like to see the flowers bloom
The stars so light and bright
But life goes on, amid this gloom
Because I have no sight.

Close your eyes, how do you feel?
It's never day or night.
I cannot use what I haven't got
Because I have no sight.

Don't pity me, I have a gift too
A world of my own, oh so bright
I can see things, just like you
Although I'll never have sight.

Lilli De Pasquale (10)
St James CE Middle School, Bury St Edmunds

DARKNESS

Darkness falls on the deer, that are grazing in the wood.
Darkness falls on the cat stalking on a red brick wall.
Darkness falls on the hedgehog, rustling through the leaves.
Darkness falls on the badger, feeding her babies.
Darkness falls on the wolf, waiting for its prey.
Darkness falls on the squirrel, burying some nuts.
Darkness falls on the wolf, howling loud and clear.
Darkness falls on me, as I come out of this dark wood.

Julia Herrington (10)
St James CE Middle School, Bury St Edmunds

THE ISLAND

We crashed on an island
To see what we could see
We didn't mean to do this
But that's what happened to me.

I looked around to see what I could see
All I could see was the sea, sea, sea.
The sea was blue, the sea was rough
That's what happened to me.

With the birds calling
The sea crashing
I didn't know what was happening
So I called around but no one answered
That's what happened to me!

Emily Long (11)
St James CE Middle School, Bury St Edmunds

MY BROTHER

My brother always hits me,
But I still love him,
My brother always pulls my hair,
But I still care,
My brother always calls me names
But still we have fun,
My brother always kisses me goodnight,
That's the part I don't like!
Then I give him one and then it starts all over again.
I do it till I'm not bothered any more.
Well he's only five!

Nicola Abbott (10)
St James CE Middle School, Bury St Edmunds

SEASONS

Winter is cold,
Cold as ice.
Ice starts to melt,
Melt ready for spring.
Spring is getting warmer,
Warmer as the flowers come out,
Out to see the sunshine
Shine everywhere.
Where summer's coming,
Coming back again,
Again we play in the sun.
Sun out from behind the clouds.
Clouds start to come back for autumn.
Autumn when leaves start to fall off the trees.
Trees start to die,
Die when the winter is coming
Coming to start the cold
Cold is winter,
Winter is cold.

Hannah Dracott (10)
St James CE Middle School, Bury St Edmunds

THE HAUNTED HOUSE

In Yorkshire once, there was a house,
And it was very grand,
But it was haunted,
And so it was deserted.

The house fell into ruin and decay,
Because nobody lived there,
Until one night in late October,
A person moved in.

He was extremely poor,
And he knew about the ghost,
But he didn't care,
And set off to work.

The ghost beckoned him with a bony finger,
He went with the ghost and then he disappeared,
When he came to the place where he disappeared,
He found a skeleton bound in chains.

Thomas Taylor (10)
St James CE Middle School, Bury St Edmunds

THE JUNGLE

Animals are here and there
There in the jungle
Jungle that is over there
There you will find me
Me the queen of the jungle
Jungle that I love.

The jungle is full of animals
Animals like gorillas
Gorillas that live in trees
Trees that have leaves
Leaves eaten by giraffes
Giraffes that are large.

Tigers are frightening
Frightening as can be
Be like a lion
Lions which roar all day
Day turns to night
Night when some sleep.

Fay Beamish (10)
St James CE Middle School, Bury St Edmunds

LOVE

Love is . . .
as hot as red spices,
Burning like
red hot volcanoes.
You can't touch love
But
The love touches you.
It's boxes of chocolates,
Red roses,
and birds whistling
In the treetops.

Holly Lowman (12)
St Louis' RC Middle School, Bury St Edmunds

DISAPPOINTMENT

Disappointment is like a grey evening.
It tastes empty, cold and bitter.
The look is of a lost puppy desperately trying
to find its mother, but later accepting defeat.
The sound of a cry of despair slicing through
the air colder than a winter's.
And it feels like you're carrying a weight
heavier than yourself.
The smell is like a musty attic.
But it's your soul pulling you down
further and further towards despair.

Shona Scanlan (12)
St Louis' RC Middle School, Bury St Edmunds

A PERFECT PICTURE

The glistening sunlight
Brightens the irresistible magic
through branches
The fingers of sunlight turn the
waters to gold
Imagination of endless waters
Cascade onwards
Animals mesmerised by the pure
beauty of the
scenic wonder
Immortal waters
Plunge down deep
Through the curtains of mist
And steam.

Anna Barnett (13)
St Louis' RC Middle School, Bury St Edmunds

IRRESISTIBLE IMMORTAL MAGIC

The scenic splendour beckons us to watch
The amazing landscapes full of sheer power and glory.
Mystic comets spinning full of spray.
Loving, emerald pool awaits.
The accelerating and leaping curtains of water.
Drenching clouds of smoke that thunders.
Filled with the tide of affairs.
The confusion of water makes it obvious.
The hand of God at work.

Kirsty Banns (13)
St Louis' RC Middle School, Bury St Edmunds

AQUATIC ALLURE

Upstream, the magic flows on silent haunches,
The mumchance incantation unfurls as the
torrent races on,
A magnitude of mystical splendour is kept
behind the falls,
Dark exsufflations meet light and plummet into
the cleansing emerald pools to unite and become one,
Fingers of enchantment embrace and besot the
unsuspecting onlooker,
Into a state of hypnotic wonderment.

Katie Dryden-Holt (13)
St Louis' RC Middle School, Bury St Edmunds

THE UNITED WATERFALL

As I prepare to plunge into oblivion,
And the adrenalin runs through my veins,
As I open my wings, my drenching heart sings,
As they gaze at me making my way.

Before I meet comrade, and shake at his waves,
I see his life welcome my smile,
Yet independence is lost,
It is just a small cost,
For I know I shall never be alone.

Clare MacKie (13)
St Louis' RC Middle School, Bury St Edmunds

THE POWER OF WATER

A spray of water
hitting the air,
like it's spreading out
its wings.
Tumbling down in a wide mass,
Shaping the land as it goes.
There's a certain sparkle
in emerald pools,
like stars twinkling in the night,
Its irresistible magic mesmerises you.
Flowing in its natural splendour
The rainbows greet the newborn river,
After a relentless confusion of water
The water gushes out in sheer
power and glory,
Like it's giving the rocks a watery baptism.
The excitement then drowns
in a magnitude of brilliance,
And the immortal river is
sparkling still in the sunlight.

Peter Cianciola (13)
St Louis' RC Middle School, Bury St Edmunds

COULD IT BE WITHIN THIS WORLD?

Could it be within this world?
With flames for red and gold, heat burns the skull,
as death can come from this burning red flame,
evil ruling, happiness lives no more.

Could it be within this world?
The frightening flames from the red burning fire?
Kill the eagle with a slit in its wing,
and death can come from this terrible thing.

Could it be within this world?
Where pink pigs will fly in the yellow sky,
Where the horses will bark and the dogs will purr,
Where famous words will be given by birds
and humans are no more than animals.

Could it be within this world?
That when someone dies, they can be reborn,
another life, another place, you can
be safe living in the most special world.

Could it be within this world?
The world we live in is optimistic,
sometimes right and sometimes wrong, you never know,
that's the way it is, the way it goes.

Abi Barnes (13)
Sir John Leman High School

MUM'S POEMS

My mum likes reading poetry,
Gets books out from the library,
She reads it line by line.
Says it's a good way to spend your time.
Then thinks I ought to listen,
As she reads aloud her favourite lines.

She recites it when I'm home from school,
Because she thinks it's really cool.
She thinks that I should read some,
Perhaps make up some rhymes.
But what could I write about?
I haven't much spare time.

Jennifer Utting (13)
Sir John Leman High School

MY NAN
(Dedicated to my beloved nanny who suffers from
the excruciating illness Myalgic Encephalomyelitis (ME))

She's a tortoise when she's moving around,
And a soft cushion to protect you from hitting the ground.
She's a log fire cosy and warm.
And a bright orange sun awakening at dawn.
She's an encyclopaedia clever and wise,
and a brand new Porsche a great surprise!
She's a tropical holiday a fantastic destination,
But when she gets tired it's like she's gone into hibernation.
If she was a landmark she'd be Stonehenge,
Still standing even though she was crumbling to her fall.
If she was a building she'd be an air raid shelter,
Because she protects everyone and is so comforting
with her reassuring call.
Her temper can only be slight like a small rain cloud
But most of the time it's like a hot summer's day
bubbly and bright.
If she was something to do with space she'd be
the brightest star in the darkest night.
Her love and cuddles are full of reassuring trust
and hope for me.
She's the best nan I ever did see.

Aneliese Rix (13)
Sir John Leman High School

SUMMER

Feel the sun warm the earth with its hot rays.
Smell the sweetness of the blossom lingering in the
air anticipating long hot summer days.
Children playing happily without a care,
Egging each other on with do or dare.
Flowers and trees swaying gently in the breeze
Wildlife abound munching on grass and weeds.
Happy days with happy thoughts and dreams,
Smiling brightly great grins and beams.
Summer nights long and sultry,
Peaceful thoughts go through one's mind.
Memories of the past move to come,
Sharing laughter and love is so much fun.
Hope for the future with family and friends,
Time to move on and make amends.
Summer is here with its warm cheerful glow,
Making the most of life and living life to the full.

Melodie Key (13)
Sir John Leman High School

LAURA

There is a girl her name is Laura
Quite frankly I adore her,
She's got dark hair, she's really fair.
I know we would make a good pair.
The thing I like most about Laura is the
Way she laughs when I bore her.
But after all she's much too tall
So I guess I'll have to stick to small.

Joseph Appleby (13)
Stradbroke High School

BOYS V GIRLS, GIRLS V BOYS

Boys are cool, girls are fair
boys are lazy girls are rare
girls wear heels boys wear trainers
boys watch football where girls watch *Neighbours.*

Richard Wittey (12)
Stradbroke High School

GIRLS

Girls are so sad all they worry
about is
hair
boys
if they look alright
And they think they are it but they are not.

Alan Hewitt (13)
Stradbroke High School

KALEIDOSCOPE

C olours blue and yellow
O r even pink and green
L inking together to make more patterns
O verwhelming colour
U p and down the patterns move
R ushing into one another.

Victoria Grigg (12)
Stradbroke High School

GIRLS V BOYZ

They're made of brains,
They're made of dirt,
But they can be sweet,
So girls can flirt.

Some are tall and dark,
Some are small and blonde,
Some are thin,
Fat,
Some are wizards with their
Magic wands.

But we love 'em to bits,
Really they're pink and full of fluff,
On the outside they try to,
Act hard and tough.

Some boys can be gentlemen,
Some are just pathetic,
But when we take the mick,
They just can't hack it.

The football comes first,
Then hopefully we come next,
Some appreciate us girls,
Some are best friends with their ex.

All in all they are softies and,
They really need a shoulder to cry on,
So give 'em a break for once in a
Lifetime give 'em some love, go on.

Laura Lee & Katie Thacker (13)
Stradbroke High School

What a Word

Kaleidoscope
What a word
It's not like a telescope
But it's the same shape.
It doesn't see the moon and far
But only down a tube
Bright red, yellow, blue.
Making green, brown, orange.
When they mix together,
That shape looks like a tree
No a cloud.
What's now a church window pattern
Kaleidoscope
What a word.

Amy Cattermole (13)
Stradbroke High School

Dream School

My dream school is so big,
The teachers have to wear funny wigs.
Instead of doing lots of work,
You can sit and act a jerk.
Sit and watch TV all day,
And let the other children go and play.
School dinners are so yummy.
They make you feel good in your tummy.
If you could do this all in one day,
You wouldn't want to go home and play.

Samantha Catling (12)
Westbourne High School

MY FIRST DAY AT SCHOOL

I got dressed to go to school,
I thought I looked a complete fool.
My heart was throbbing like a dog,
I thought I would just lie in bed
As still as a log.
I was too excited to get up again,
But I had to in the end.
I had the butterflies on the way to school,
People were staring, they think they're so cool.
I went outside at break and had fun,
Playing in the lovely sun.
Then we went into DT.
Then we went to PE.
We played netball.
And I tumbled down with a great fall.
Everyone was laughing,
I had badly hurt my chin,
I was so upset,
I felt the tears running down my face,
They were wet.
At lunchtime I had egg, chips, pizza and cheese,
I said, 'Thank you' and 'please.'
At home time I told my mum,
How Westbourne was so much fun.
I felt jiggly, wiggly inside
I wanted to run and hide.

Tara Sorhaindo (12)
Westbourne High School

LATE NIGHTS OUT

In the morning when the sun is rising you've just come back from a late night out. You're lying in bed and your head is thumping, your feet are aching and your stomach pumping.

Your dad told you to be in by eleven, you didn't come back until half past seven. Just what is he going to say now, is it going to end in a row?

I hope not I said as I dragged myself out of bed, my head was thumping and I felt as if I was dead.

Laura Rudge (12)
Westbourne High School